Jews and Christians
in a
Pluralistic World

Jews and Christians
in a
Pluralistic World

EDITED BY
ERNST-WOLFGANG BÖCKENFÖRDE
& EDWARD SHILS

ST. MARTIN'S PRESS
NEW YORK

© 1991 Institut für die Wissenschaften vom
Menschen

All rights reserved. For information, write:
Scholarly and Reference Division,
St. Martin's Press, Inc., 175 Fifth Avenue,
New York, NY 10010

First published in the United States of America
in 1991

Printed in Great Britain

ISBN 0-312-07268-6

Library of Congress Cataloging-in-Publication

Jews and Christians in a pluralistic world
edited by Ernst-Wolfgang Böckenförde and
Edward Shils.
p.   cm.

ISBN 0-312-07268-6

1. Judaism–Relations–Christianity.
2. Christianity and other religions–Judaism.
3. Christianity and antisemitism.
I. Böckenförde, Ernst Wolfgang.
II. Shils, Edward Albert, 1911–
BM536.J48   1991
261.2′ 6–dc20

91–29165
CIP

CONTENTS

v

Contents

NOTES ON CONTRIBUTORS

Cardinal Dr Franz König was born in 1905 in Rabenstein/Pielach. He is an Austrian ecclesiastic who studied at the universities of Rome, Lille and Vienna and was ordained in 1933. He was Docent at Vienna University in 1946; Professor at the Faculty of Theology in Salzburg in 1948; Titular Bishop of Livinas in 1952; Archbishop of Vienna, 1956–85; and created Cardinal by Pope John XXIII in 1958.

He is the author of *Glaube in Freiheit* (1981), *Der Glaube der Menschen* (1985), *Der Weg der Kirche* (1986), *Lexikon der Religionen* (1987) and *Juden und Christen haben eine Zukunft* (1983).

R. J. Zwi Werblowsky was born in 1924 and educated in London and Geneva. After teaching at the University of Leeds and the Institute of Jewish Studies in Manchester he moved in 1956 to the Hebrew University of Jerusalem where he is Martin Buber Professor of Comparative Religion. He has taken up numerous visiting professorships: in Harvard, Chicago, Stanford, Notre-Dame, Melbourne and Tokyo. From 1975 to 1985 he was Secretary-General of the International Association for the History of Religions and since 1984 has been Vice President of the Conseil International de Philosophie et des Sciences Humaines.

His publications focus particularly on Jewish mysticism and the religions of the Far East. He is co-editor of the journal *Numen*.

Geza Vermes was born in 1924 and was educated in Budapest and Louvain. After holding a post as Senior Lecturer at Newcastle he became Reader in Jewish Studies at the Oriental Institute of the University of Oxford, a post he has held since 1965. He has been Chairman of the Curators of the Oriental Institute in Oxford, is Professorial Fellow of Wolfson College, Oxford and became Fellow of the British Academy in 1985. He has held numerous guest professorships and has been editor of the *Journal of Jewish Studies* since 1971.

His publications include *The Gospel of Jesus the Jew* (1981) and *The Dead Sea Scrolls Forty Years On* (1987).

Aleksander Gieysztor was born in 1916 in Moscow and educated at the University of Warsaw where he was made professor in 1949. He was Director of the Historical Institute there from 1955 to 1975 and has been President of the International Committee of Historical Sciences since 1980. He has held visiting research posts at the universities of Oxford and Harvard and is a member of many learned societies. He is Director of the Royal Castle in Warsaw and Deputy Chairman of the Advisory Board of the IWM.

His publications focus on Polish history with special reference to the Middle Ages and include *Genesis of the Crusades* (1950), *History of Poland* (1968), *Thousand Years of Poland* (1976) and numerous articles on medieval history.

Jacob Katz was born in 1904 in Magyargencs (Hungary) and studied history and sociology. In 1936 he emigrated to Palestine, becoming Docent at the Hebrew University in Jerusalem in 1959, then Professor at the Hebrew University in 1962, and from 1969–72 Rector of the University.

He is the author of *Zur Assimilisation und Emanzipation der Juden. Ausgewählte Schriften* (1982), *Aus dem Ghetto in die bürgerliche Gesellschaft. Jüdische Emanzipation 1770–1870* (1986) and *Vom Vorurteil bis zur Vernichtung. Der Antisemitismus 1700–1933* (1989).

Jan Błoński was born in 1931 in Warsaw and studied at the University of Cracow. As a literary critic, he was active in the cultural reawakening of the years 1956–60 (*Poeci i inni*, 1956, *Zmiana warty*, 1961). After a few years in Paris and the publication of *M. Sep Szarzynski and the Origins of the Polish Baroque* (1967), he returned to Cracow in 1969. He is Director of the Institute for Polish Philology at the Jagellonian University, Cracow, and a Corresponding Member of the IWM.

While continuing his critical work (*Odmarsz*, 1977), Błoński dedicated himself primarily to the study of the works of Witkiewicz and Gombrowicz. In 1971 he became co-founder and editor of *Teksty* (banned in 1981), a literary journal aimed at injecting a new spirit into Polish literary investigation. With regard to French literature Błoński has published two books, one on Proust (1964) and one on Beckett (1982). He has also translated Artaud and Barthes into Polish. Following *Romans e Teksteur* (1981), he published a collection of essays in 1983, *Kilka mysli co nie nowe*, on the current problems of Polish culture and literature.

Jozef Tischner is the President of the Institut für die Wissenschaften vom Menschen. He is Professor of Human Philosophy on the Papal Faculty for Theology in Cracow. He has been the Deacon of the Philosophical Faculty at the Papal Theological Academy in Cracow since 1982.

His publications include *Etyka solidarnosci* (1981), *Polski ksztalt dialogu* (1981), *Christentum und Marxismus in Polen* (1982), *Myslenie wedlug war-*

tosci (1982) and *Das menschliche Drama. Phänomenologische Studien zur Philosophie des Dramas* (1989).

Owen Chadwick was born in 1916 in England and was educated at the University of Cambridge. He taught history there from 1947 to 1983, being Regius Professor of Modern History from 1968–83, Vice-Chancellor of the University from 1969–71 and Master of Selwyn College from 1956–83. He was President of the British Academy from 1981–85 and has numerous honorary degrees. He was knighted in 1982 and is now Regius Professor Emeritus of Modern History at the University of Cambridge.

He is the author of *The Victorian Church* (2 volumes, 1966–70). He has been much concerned with the relationship between the Christian churches and the changing science of history in the nineteenth century, being the author of *The Secularization of the European Mind* (1975) and investigating the way in which historical ideals led to the opening of the Vatican Archives by Pope Leo XIII in *Catholicism and History* (1978). As a background to the Catholic nineteenth century he wrote *The Popes and European Revolution* (1981). His most recent publications are *Britain and the Vatican during the Second World War* (1987), *From Bossuet to Newman* (1987), *Michael Ramsey. A Life* (1990) and *The Spirit of the Oxford Movement. Tractarian Essays* (1990).

Ernst-Wolfgang Böckenförde was born in Kassel in 1930. He obtained the degrees of Doctor of Law from the University of Münster in 1956 and Doctor of Philosophy from the University of Munich in 1961. He has been Professor of Law at the universities of Heidelberg (1964–69) and Bielefeld (1969–77) and at Freiburg i. Br. since 1977. He has been a judge at the Federal Constitutional Court of Germany since December 1983 and is Chairman of the Advisory Board of the IWM.

His main research areas are state and constitutional law and theory, the history of constitutions, and the relation of state, church and politics. His publications include *Demokratie und Repräsentation* (1983), *Der deutsche Katholizismus im Jahre 1933. Kirche und demokratisches Ethos* (1988), *Religionsfreiheit. Die Kirche in der modernen Welt* (1990) and *State, Liberty, Society* (1991).

Edward Shils, born in 1910, is Professor of Social Thought and Sociology at the University of Chicago and Honorary Fellow of Peterhouse at the University of Cambridge. He is Deputy Chairman of the Advisory Board of the IWM.

His most recent publications include *The Calling of Sociology* (1980), *Tradition* (1981), *The Constitution of Society* (1982) and *The Academic Ethic* (1983).

Rabbi Leon Klenicki is Director of the Department of Jewish–Catholic Relations, Anti-Defamation League of B'nai B'rith. He is editor of *Face* to Face: *An Interreligious Bulletin* and teaches at the Immaculate Conception Seminary, New Jersey, on rabbinic Judaism and early Christianity and Jewish understanding of Christianity from rabbinic times to the twentieth century.

He is co-editor of *A Dictionary of Jewish–Christian Dialogue* (1984) and *Pope John Paul II on Jews and Judaism 1979–1986* (1987).

Pietro Rossano was born in 1923. After studying literature, theology and the history of religion he taught at the Pontifical universities of Gregory, Urban and the Lateran University from 1953 to 1965. In that year he became Secretary of the Papal Commission for the Vulgate Bible, a post he held until 1971. In 1973 he became Secretary of the Vatican division for non-Christian religions and in 1983 Pope John Paul II made him suffragan bishop of Rome for culture and also Rector of the Pontifical Lateran University there.

His publications include: *Vangelo e cultura* (1985) and *I perche dell'uomo e le risposte delle grandi religioni* (1988). He is chairman of the Catholic and Jewish editorial board of the *Classici delle religioni*.

INTRODUCTION

From 28 to 30 November 1988, three weeks after the fiftieth anniversary of the *Reichspogromnacht* of 1938, a conference was held in Vienna on the subject of 'Jews and Christians in a Pluralistic World'. It was organized by the Vienna Institut für die Wissenschaften vom Menschen (Institute for Human Sciences).

Why such a conference, and what did it set out to achieve? Meetings between Christians and Jews to discuss the relations between them in the past and present are still fraught with difficulties, notwithstanding the sincere efforts made on both sides. This is particularly true when such discussions, beyond providing personal contacts or purely academic contacts, are held in public between persons who speak in their capacity as Jews and as Christians. The reason is obvious. Nevertheless, such meetings are necessary. Particularly after the burdens of the past and the inconceivably horrible events of the Holocaust, Jews and Christians share common tasks and common responsibility for living together with mutual respect. They also find themselves in pluralistic civil societies such as are now spreading from the West into Central and Eastern Europe. Together they face many problems which they deal with as citizens of their own societies and of the larger world beyond the boundaries of their own religious communities and their own national societies. They must jointly deal with problems of social and political action.

Meetings of this kind can bear fruit only if they tread the right path. That path must not avoid the manifold potential and actual conflicts and tensions that have long characterized the relations between Jews and Christians with a background of the stresses and strains of the past and the difficult issues that these raise. The old Jewish adage quoted by President Richard von Weizsäcker,[1] 'the secret of redemption is called memory', applies here too: there can be no atonement without remembrance. What has stood and still stands between Christians and Jews and the memory of the things that have happened in the course of the history of the Jews as a minority in predominantly Christian societies can lead to an understanding, possibly even to a reconciliation, *only* if they are not covered up but are courageously and thoroughly dealt with, root and branch. It must not be forgotten – indeed, it needs to be brought out into the open and discussed – that the instigators and agents of the Holocaust were not heathens or 'barbarians' but were for the most part men and women who had been baptized as Christians.

Thanks to the open-mindedness of those who first proposed it and the confidence of willingness on both sides, the conference set out on this path of free encounter, tackling the problems without reservations. The location of the conference in Vienna and the topics with which it dealt bore eloquent testimony to this.

Vienna is a city that for Jews in particular is associated with mixed memories – memories of a heyday of a relatively free existence and intellectual and cultural achievements under the Habsburg monarchy in the decades prior to the First World War. Vienna is also a city which calls forth memories of the accompanying budding, burgeoning and ultimately rampant anti-Semitism that created a fertile climate for the coming of the Holocaust. The choice of Vienna, of all places, as the location for the encounter and enlisting the participation of persons of standing and authority were bold moves, indicative of a genuine readiness to embark on a dialogue. They were not without their effect.[2]

The topics discussed at the conference did not attempt to avoid the problems and difficulties on both sides. Attention was directed, on the one hand, to the common historical roots of the Christian and Jewish religions, by virtue of which they are related in a specific manner – through their profession of faith in God, which is something they also have in common with Islam. This needs to be acknowledged and accepted and, if possible, lifted out of a controversial interpretation; and this must be done with a view to exploring how both religions, each of which makes its own distinctive claim excluding the other to represent the truth, may nonetheless enjoy positive relations or simply coexist side by side. On the other hand, the conference looked at how Christians and Jews have seen each other throughout history, often on the basis of prejudices, animosities and misunderstandings, and at the conflict-laden relations that ensued. The process began with the argument about the significance of Jesus's Jewishness and continued with the distorted perceptions that each side has had of the other since Medieval times and their consequences, up to and including the attempts made in the eighteenth and nineteenth centuries to emancipate the Jews and the unfulfilled – possibly unfulfillable – expectation to which those attempts gave rise. It was the opposition to that emancipation that helped to bring about modern anti-Semitism.

The question arises of how far the penetrating analysis offered by Jan Błoński in the present volume,[3] vividly and straightforwardly referring to Polish Roman Catholic opinion, exposes the foundations of the misperception of the attitudes of Christians towards Jews: namely, spiritual anti-Judaism which sees and represents the Jews as enemies of the people of God, which they extended into social and political hostility, and which thus inevitably turns into an existential tension and even outright contradiction of the Christian Commandment to see the Jews as fellow men and women – as neighbours, in fact – and to treat them accordingly. Is it not this spiritual anti-Judaism, which Christians have had inculcated in them for generations, that accounts specifically for the widespread passivity of Christians in the face of nascent and mounting hostility to, and persecution of, Jews? This spiritual anti-Judaism raises the questions of whether the tradition of *polis*-religion in Christianity, which sees the Jews as enemies of God's people, is in conflict with the substance of Christian belief and with the mission of Christianity as a universal religion embracing benevolence towards, and love of, all men without exception.

Then there are the common tasks and responsibilities that Jews and Christians have in and for the world, but these cannot be thought about in isolation from the obligation of working through our mutual understandings and misunderstandings, with all their face-flung ramifications. The prospect that these tasks and responsibilities will be acknowledged and accepted as joint tasks and responsibilities is founded, on the one hand, on the postulate of Christian humanitarianism and a corresponding commitment to the Jews, which in the context of the Holocaust, particularly, was enhanced by the tone and content of the discussions in Vienna. Optimism is supported by the new attitude towards religious freedom that has in the meantime come to prevail in the Christian churches, including the Roman Catholic church. By virtue of the principle of religious freedom which forms part of it, the political order of civil society, based on the recognition of human rights, equality before the law and the separation of powers, prevents religion as such or any particular religion from determining the political character of the nation or of the state. Religion is set free, but it is also kept free; it does not, *qua* religion, constitute an essential, obligatory component of the general order. In acknowledging religious freedom in this sense – that is to say, as an external right within the orbit of the state – the Christian churches and the Jews have also erected a landmark as regards their relations with each other. This has had repercussions on the reassessment of their common history.[4] The external right of the other party to exist is no longer questioned. In view of this, a foundation of trust is now being laid. This infuses a different quality into the controversies. Religious belief, losing its political and social aggressiveness, can become a search for truth in freedom. At the same time, we can now see what epoch-making importance attaches to the declaration of the Second Vatican Council concerning religious freedom. It is only against this background that the substantive implications of what the Council had to say about the relationship between Christians and Jews becomes clear.

Consequently, it is now becoming possible for Christians and Jews to speak without private reservations of 'achievements and unfinished agenda' in the Judeo-Christian relationship. The two sides can start to put their heads together to see how the belief in God that Jews and Christians jointly profess may be kept alive and defended in the secular context of the civil society – and how, too, the concern, supported by that belief, to sustain and defend the world as God's creation may be made reality, and the poverty that reigns in many parts of the world may at last be brought under control.

The conference initiated a dialogue on this subject too, and it should be continued. Perhaps the dialogue still lacks the requisite impartiality and urgency. But that kind of impartiality, that kind of urgency as a bridge to joint action must, after the events of the Holocaust, be given time to grow. It seems to us that the conference in Vienna made an important contribution to the strengthening of this bridge.

Ernst-Wolfgang Böckenförde and Edward Shils *

NOTES

[1] In his speech to the German Bundestag on 8 May 1985, the fortieth anniversary of the surrender.

[2] See B. Anderson in the *Sunday Telegraph* of 4 December 1988.

[3] See below pp. 72–7.

[4] J. Messner, 'Judenschema / Religionsfreiheit', in *Die Furche* 49 (1965), p. 9.

* The editors are very grateful to Klaus Nellen for his attention to detail in preparing this volume for publication.

I

THE FUNDAMENTAL QUESTIONS

The Common Roots of the Jewish and Christian Religions

CARDINAL FRANZ KÖNIG

Our discussions here will take place in the context of the pluralistic society of our time. I mean by this the multiplicity of political interests and groups, voluntary associations, religious denominations and philosophies of life. This social and cultural complexity has taken shape in the course of development of our secular and industrial society. The unifying values of a pluralistic society are basic values such as human rights and toleration. Toleration thus has an ever growing importance today as the recognition of and respect for others, and their intellectual and religious views.

Toleration, it should be emphasized, is not to be confused with relativism, which means the devaluation and levelling of differing beliefs and philosophies. Toleration means respecting others and learning from them. Relativism, by contrast, means the attempt on both sides to make all values match those of the other – with the result that everyone's standards are lowered. In our day this relativism has led to a lessening of the importance, and this means the influence, of religion in the lives of human beings. In other words, the religious aspect – whatever is meant by that – comes to be valued less, or is given a lower status in public opinion which is much affected by the media. Adherents of both Jewish and Christian faiths must be aware of such a trend. Our common task must therefore be to encourage respectful toleration, not the relativism which is the product of religious indifference.

Perhaps the dialogue between the Jewish religious community and the Catholic church has not generated as much interest recently as it did during the last Vatican Council. Yet, in my view, the results since Vatican II have been both positive and enduring; the mutual mistrust of many centuries has been reduced, anti-Semitism condemned and now there is dialogue where there was once only monologue – surely this constitutes a revolution in the relationship between Jews and Christians in this century. Even more important for Christians is the new recognition that the roots of Christianity, of the church itself, reach back to the intellectual and spiritual world of the patriarchs, Moses and the prophets – for many Catholics this has been a ground-breaking discovery. Discovering the common roots of the two religions in this way has given Christians a clearer insight into Judaism, and at the same time we have been helped to a better understanding of some of the more mysterious aspects of our own faith.

This certainly does not involve any new interpretation of the common spiritual heritage of Judaism and Christianity. Our meeting confirms that Jews and Christians, for the first time in history, have *come together* in order to recognize their common and distinct if not quite separate religious and historic mission at a time of radical change. There is a new kind of hope in our pluralistic society. With it a new spiritual force has appeared, which will hearten all those who are fearful and uncertain in a world where there is terrorism and war-threatening political tensions, a world of injustice and enmity. Acknowledging and affirming our common spiritual heritage may mean much more for the devout representatives of Jews and Christians in our pluralistic society than is generally supposed, or than we ourselves think.

Against the background of our present spiritual situation, I will try now to put the common roots of our religion in a larger frame.

It is not my task here to repeat what was said in *Nostra aetate* 4 of the Second Vatican Council. This short but signifi-

cant text has been the subject of many commentaries, and
has been interpreted by bishops' conferences on various
occasions. I might mention here, apart from the Austrian
bishops' conference, the texts of the German bishops' conference, and above all the declaration by the French bishops
of April 1973. I would especially like to mention here the
'extraordinary contributions', as Rabbi Klenicki has described
them, of Pope John Paul II. He has, in roughly thirty speeches
given on various occasions, such as the visit to the synagogue
in Rome, said much to encourage greatly our historic dialogue. This has prompted the church to deliberate repeatedly
on 'its own mystery', on the spiritual ties of Christians to
the tribe of Abraham, the idea that the Christian faith has
its roots in the patriarchs, in Moses and in the prophets –
these are all theological interpretations of great importance
for Christian self-understanding, and hence for Christian
identity. Thus anti-Judaism and anti-Semitism, with all their
awful consequences, and the idea of the collective guilt of
the Jews for Christ's crucifixion, have not only been rejected
for humanitarian reasons, but also, and above all, their rejection has been grounded more deeply and effectively in the
religious motive itself.

A second point: when we speak of the common roots which
join together our communities of faith, we should put much
more emphasis on monotheism – the belief in one God –
than has hitherto been the case. According to Mark the evangelist 12, 29, Jesus was asked which commandment was the
first above all others. In his reply, he repeated the sentence
from Deuteronomy 6,4: 'Hear, O Israel, the Lord our God
is one Lord. And thou shalt love the Lord thy God with all
thy heart, and with all thy soul, and with all thy mind, and
with all thy strength.' This, so often quoted, is proof that
the young Christian communities took the concept of the
divine, in the sense of Christ's teaching, from the Old Testament without alteration. At this point I do not wish to discuss
in detail the Christian doctrine of the Trinity as an explanation
of God's historical act of salvation in Jesus Christ, for the

Christian faith professes the unity of God in the community of the Father, the Son and the Holy Ghost; it therefore stands firmly on the ground of monotheism.

In other respects, the concept of monotheism has become more complex in our era. In the nineteenth century and the first half of the twentieth century, the Old Testament came, under the influence of rationalism, to be more and more regarded as a source text which could be used by historians to show how Israel developed from polytheism to strict monotheism. The state of theological studies in those days meant that the books of the Old Testament could be seen as revealing a religious evolution from polytheism, by way of a form of henotheism, to an at first uncertain, but then distinct, monotheism. Social, political and economic factors were seen as decisive in this progression. At the same time, however, the religious approach to the Bible, to Israel and thus also Christianity was obstructed. I might mention here, from the beginning of this century, such names as Adolf von Harnack, Julius Wellhausen and the Orientalist Franz Delitzsch. A Protestant theologian and church historian, von Harnack, who died in 1930, provides one interesting example. In his book on *Marcion* of the second century he argued that the reformers of the sixteenth century had been unable to bring themselves to reject the Old Testament as Marcion had done in the second century. However, he continued, 'To make a clean sweep of all this, and to honour truth both in doctrine and teachings, that is the great deed which today, almost too late, is demanded of Protestantism.'[1] This devaluation of the Old Testament is accompanied by anti-Judaic and later anti-Semitic remarks. The young Hegel had already called the God of the Old Testament a 'demon of hatred'. Franz Delitzsch, who died in 1922, was the instigator of the Babylon Bible (Bibel–Babel) controversy, and the founder of Pan-Babylonianism. He was of the opinion that the Christian church could completely dispense with the Old Testament. Or, as he wrote himself: 'The often heard, and sentimental, statement, that Judaism brought forth the world's redemption, should for all time give way to the historically much less dubious claim that it was Judaism which killed the world's redeemer.' In our time it was only with the figure of Dietrich Bonhoeffer that the tide turned. Even today it is still up to us to continue to inform and explain, so that the Old Testament is accepted as a matter of course, just as much as it was among the first generations of Christians. It must no longer be regarded exclusively as a source for the history of religion. In this way, the religious approach to it will be cleared once again, as it was championed and defended from the beginning by religious Judaism and the whole of Christianity. In this way, we can clearly affirm that the monotheism of the Israelites is neither the fruit of metaphysical reflection, nor of political integration, nor of religious evolution. It is simply a statement of belief, and is therefore as old as the faith of Israel itself, that is to say the conviction of its chosenness – that is, the conviction that Israel has been chosen from all the peoples by God to convey this belief to all mankind, as it was understood from the beginning by Christianity, and adopted by it.[2]

Our spiritual heritage, as it was formed by Biblical monotheism, works from the past into the future. In the interest of the future of all mankind we should not just be aware of this, but should also open our minds more fully to its influence. For a universal and complete system of thought is connected with the Biblical concept of God. Our God is Father and Creator of all mankind, which is on its way to Him in a just and peaceful world order. Contemporary religious-historical and philosophical discussions of monotheism have made it clear that the Biblical concept of God, which is indeed our common heritage and its root, has become a central idea of the Western world. The idea of monotheism as a divine reality has indeed, in past centuries, affected and influenced the religious thought of all mankind.

At the same time, we have seen how dangerous secular surrogates are. If an individual human being kills the God of our revelation in order to put himself in his place, terrible things happen. There is the example of Friedrich Nietzsche, who pioneered the way for National Socialism with his racial theories. The secular Marxist utopia is another example, in its attempt to turn the Christian image of mankind upside down by dictatorial principles, replacing the Biblical God with a deified state. I point too to the cultural relevance of Biblical monotheism with regard to culture and society. Richard Niebuhr has argued that the monotheistic influence on society, with its principles of equality and fraternity, has lost ground to henotheistic views.[3] (In this context I think I should mention that Jewish as well as Muslim writers have also emphasized the importance of a radical monotheism as a direct or indirect critique of the polytheistic – that is, the atheistic and henotheistic tendencies in modern society.) Certain social groups have tried to become the central focus of the value systems of their respective societies and they have laid exclusive claims to the loyalty of those societies. In 1935 Erik Peterson, in his often quoted book *Monotheismus als politisches Problem*, described the belief in one God as the foundation of a political ideology which encouraged totalitarian tendencies.[4] Leaders of the new right in France have been trying to make the monotheistic world view, as a kind of ideology, responsible for the repression of human freedom and for forcing so many people to turn to atheism as the only alternative. Similarly David Miller has expressed the view that creativity and modern culture require a return to the sources of polytheism.[5] Representatives of a rationalized theology point to the way in which Biblical monotheism is biased toward a one-sidedly patriarchal way of thinking.

In contrast to these one-sided and rationalistic views, it is to the credit of a man such as Bernard-Henri Lévy that he has reopened the way back to Jewish tradition, and thus made us understand how the monotheistic concept of God can have such a liberating function in society. It is exactly in this basic religious idea that we have a defence against the various forms of totalitarianism and all its ideological surrogates.

The history of the religion of the Jews, of the Christians and of Islam is more than Biblical criticism and comparative theology. It is the living witness of the religious, historical and living reality of the one God, who has spoken to so many generations through the law and the prophets. This testimony is unique in the history of the religions of humanity, and confirms that, as far as is known, there has been no other such tradition in the history of mankind, which is free of polytheistic and, above all, dualistic interpretations and myths.

At this point, however, I would like not only to stress the Biblical belief in God, as something which above all else Jews and Christians have in common; and to understand this in its uniqueness as the historical root of our spiritual affinity, the foundation for our dialogue and mutual respect. Briefly I would also like to sketch once again the effects of this conviction of faith on both the individual and on society.

Fundamentally, our understanding of man is formed, even in our pluralistic society, by the monotheistic belief in God as it appears in Scripture. God is the Creator and Father of mankind, who tells them: God created man in His image, as man and woman created He them, as it appears in the well-known passage in Genesis. This is the basis of the concept of the dignity of man, of the fundamental equality and the inalienability of the rights of all human beings. Hence Jesus, when answering the question as to the most important commandment, also referred to the Book of Deuteronomy 6, 5: 'And thou shalt love the Lord thy God with all thine heart, and with all thy soul, and with all thy might.' He then adds that the second commandment is as important, and he quotes Leviticus 19, 18: 'and thy neighbour as thyself'. It was through the chosen people of Israel, then the message of Jesus of Nazareth, that this concept of God and man was to reach the whole world.

When, however, man deifies himself, he becomes in the process, the enemy of man. That has been inscribed into the history of mankind through the philosophy of Nietzsche,

9

through the racial theory of National Socialism, with its terrible consequences. Man as created by God is free and responsible for himself and his world, and a displacement of personal responsibility onto a collective entity also has fateful consequences: the flight from responsibility is also a transgression of the Biblical concept of man.

Our monotheistic belief in God, according to Scripture, reveals the world to us as God's creation. He has, however, given the world over to man's care not in order for him to exploit it, but rather for him to protect it. I am reminded of Genesis 1, 28: 'And God blessed them [man and woman], and God said unto them, "Be fruitful, and multiply, and replenish the earth, and subdue it: and have dominion over the fish of the sea, and over the fowl of the air, and over every living thing that moveth upon the earth."' That suggests the general responsibility of all mankind. It also indicates that the task can only be successfully undertaken together, in justice and peace.

Through the belief in the creation of heaven and earth we are not tied to a cyclical view of the world, but rather a linear concept of the world and of time is revealed to us. Eternal recurrence is replaced by an eschatological perspective. History is not a progression into nothingness, but rather has a conscious goal. Heidegger and Bloch are open to criticism in this respect.

With such brief references to the effects of the idea of God and the faith bound to that idea, I wanted to make clear how far-reaching are the influences that have had such an impact over the ages on the history of man in society. Every departure from the Biblical concept of man, whether in the form of an extreme individualism or a one-sided collectivism, has led historically to terrible catastrophes. I do not know how a world order of peace can be built in the future without attention being paid to religion and the Bible.

The concept of man and of the world which is based on the Biblical belief in God has its roots, its common roots, in the knowledge of, and belief in, God. In conclusion, I would like to recall the description of God given to us by Isaiah 40, 13ff.:

Who hath directed the Spirit of the Lord, or being his counsellor hath taught him?
With whom took he counsel and who instructed him, and taught him in the path of judgment, and taught him knowledge, and shewed him the way of understanding?
Behold the nations are as a drop of a bucket, and are counted as the small dust of the balance: behold, he taketh up the isles as a very little thing . . .
All nations before him are as nothing: and they are counted to him less than nothing, and vanity.
To whom then will ye liken God? Or what likeness will ye compare unto him?

Translated from the German by Steven Beller

NOTES

[1] See *Neue Zürcher Zeitung*, 4 November 1988, p. 39.
[2] See a work by French theologians, also published in German, *Wörterbuch zur biblischen Botschaft*, 1964, pp. 280ff.
[3] See the famous book by H. Richard Niebuhr, *A radical monotheism and Western culture*, New York, 1960.
[4] See E. Peterson, *Der Monotheismus als politisches Problem*, Leipzig, 1935.
[5] See D. Miller, *The New Polytheism*, 1981.

The Common Roots of Judaism and Christianity

R.J.ZWI WERBLOWSKY

My brief is both delicate and explosive. I have been asked to examine the *common roots* (plural) of Judaism and Christianity. It is a tricky situation: when, especially at the opening session of our conference, a student of religions is invited to express himself on a highly theological topic – because presumably rather more is expected of me than a lecture on historical events. However, this awkward situation has advantages. After all, the student of religion is trained to slip his feet into other people's theological shoes, as it were, and attempt to reconstruct their theological thinking. It is in this capacity, rather than, for example, as a spokesman for Judaism or Jewish theology, that I stand before you today.

It goes without saying that the scholar would prefer not to confine his attention to Judaism and Christianity. Nowadays both the study of religion and theology are characterized by an increasingly 'ecumenical' awareness. I should like to make very clear here for the student of religion the recent dialogic tendency of theology is also of enormous importance. How one religion behaves toward other religions, how and what it thinks about the 'other' – the whole *theologia religionum*, in other word – is an essential part of the self-understanding of every religion and of what it says about itself. However, this would lead me away from the theme to which I have been assigned, since Judaism and Christianity have

quite different approaches to the problem of 'other' religions
– that is, to the problem of the *oikoumene*. I shall, therefore,
more *nolens* than *volens*, confine my attention to Judaism
and Christianity.

Not only historians of religion but theologians, too, have
adopted the sometimes rather unhelpful practice of speaking
of a mother- and a daughter-religion and referring to Christianity's roots (both historical and intellectual) in Judaism.
nied by certain dangers. As well as designating, it can also
distort. Sometimes it is a light, sometimes a will-o'-the-wisp.
The early Christian community was indubitably a Jewish sect
of which there were so many at that time. When it became
the church, the mother-religion was reduced to the Old Testament, called *praeparatio evangelica*, and at best esteemed in
that role. Whatever came after the *Tanach* was regarded as
decay. The period of the Second Temple, which is what it
is called in Jewish historical writing, is not considered in
Christian historiography to be an authentically creative
efflorescence but a lengthy hiatus – the 'inter-testamentary
period', as it is called in English. The daughter swallowed
Though not wholly arbitrary, this terminology is accompathe
mother, and this was followed by the search for explanations
as to why post-Biblical Judaism nevertheless continued to
exist. Judaism was no longer looked upon as a proper tree
at all but a dead branch. The genuine tree of life was at best
the Old Testament trunk onto which the truly decisive New
Testament was grafted. The facts of the case might be graphi-
cally represented as follows: the *via regia* ran from Adam
to Abraham, Moses and David, then by way of the prophets
to Jesus and from there through the apostles to the church
of today; Judaism had turned off the main road, as it were,
and moved into a dead end. A Jew would trace the line differently: Adam, Abraham, Moses, David, prophets, scribes and
Pharisees, the Talmud, rabbinic, cabbalistic and modern
Judaism down to the present, and then from the present to
the Day of Judgement. From this main road, side roads
frequently branched off: Samaritans, Nazarene Christians,

Karaites and so on. That occasionally a side road has attained world historical significance matters little for my topic today. Or does a Christian theologian see it as significant in salvationary history that, of the dozens of Indian sects founded around the fifth century BC, some disappeared completely, (the Ajivikas, for example) while others became narrowly confined religious communities (the Jains, for example) and only Buddhism became one of the great world religions?

In any case if we are going to talk about roots or even common roots, we must take seriously this problem of perspective. For this reason, I must dwell briefly on the analogy with Buddhism. The fact is that, if we are talking about mother- and daughter-religions, we cannot help thinking of the relationship between Hinduism and Buddhism (strictly speaking, Hinduism did not exist at the time of the Buddha; we should properly speak about Vedic or Upanishadic or Brahmanical religion.) Buddhism was a critical, not to say rebellious, daughter-religion, which had its roots in Upanishadic thinking but clearly separated itself from it. Upanishadic religion, though not Buddhism itself, was rooted in Vedic religion, which, for our present purposes, we can ignore. In India, of course, the problems of those claims to exclusiveness and absolute validity are rather different. Still, it is interesting to observe that, whatever the historian might say, Buddhism regards itself as wholly independent of Hinduism, whereas Hinduism, as the mother-religion, either simply dismisses the daughter-religion as a heresy or tries to swallow it. According to Radhakrishnan and other modern neo-Hindu thinkers, the Buddha was no more and no less than a great – if wayward and original – Upanishadic thinker. In Indian terms, he was even one of the divine avatars. You can imagine how orthodox Buddhists react to these well-meaning expressions of 'ecumenical' Hinduism.

But let us, after this not entirely irrelevant digression, return to our subject. Here it is a case of the daughter swallowing up the mother, while the latter will have nothing to do with the former. Rather than being the mother's heiress, the daughter seeks to disinherit her. For the Christian the Old Testament is the promise, the New the fulfilment; the Old Testament is shadow, the New Testament reality: *Novum pascha novae legis/Phase vetus terminat.* The 'inter-testamentary' period does show a few lines of connection, but rabbinic Judaism is not even worth a mention. For non-Marcionite Christianity, Jesus was the Christ because, according to the promise, he sprang *e radice Jesse*, just as the New Testament had its roots in the Old. To the Jew, on the other hand, Christianity was and is about as relevant as are the Mormons, say, for a Catholic theologian. The not inconsiderable polemical literature that emerged among the Jews was the product not of any inner theological necessity but – after the early centuries, at least – of the compelling situation of a threatened and persecuted minority. In the Middle Ages, the 'common root' played no part whatever. In contrast to the present situation, it was Judaism and Islam that felt akin to each other. Although the Jews believed that the Muslims followed a false prophet, they were at least thought to be true monotheists rather than poorly disguised pagans, (Trinity, Mariolatry, image worship, sacramental teaching). The main difference between the dispute with Islam on the one hand and that with Christianity on the other lay in the fact that the former, in the absence of a common holy book, was necessarily detached and philosophical in tone, while the latter always had a fundamentally exegetical character.

The change in this situation in modern times and its background are our proper subject here today, because the relationship between Judaism and Christianity now faces a completely new situation. Before we turn to this, however, one further point needs to be made. Although the appraisal of Christianity by Islam and Judaism as briefly outlined above appears from today's standpoint to have been inadequate, it should be said that in the framework of Medieval thought it was wholly legitimate, even if one decisive difference must not be overlooked. The Christian–Muslim dispute was, for the West at least, a genuine polemic; the Christian–Jewish dispute was, for the Jews, at least by implication, a matter of life and death. The fact that in modern times the discussion has occasionally been based on a fresh and higher evaluation of Christianity by Judaism is one aspect of the turning-point already mentioned. This change has been given a further impetus when it has coincided with a seriously mistaken appraisal and misrepresentation of Islam. (One may use as an example Franz Rosenzweig, whose error in this respect is perhaps to be attributed less to his ignorance of Islam than to his dependence on Hegel.)

Let us go back to Judaism and Christianity. Neither religion can give up its claim to absoluteness, even where, given the ethnic rootedness of Judaism, or rather (to put it even more plainly), given the sacramental nature of the covenant with the seed of Abraham *kata sarka*, Judaism needs to define that claim differently from the way Christianity does. The claim to universality – and what some extol as religious universalism others call religious imperialism – and the claim to absoluteness are not the same. The second is possible without the first. Orthodox Hinduism cannot proselytize because a person has to be born into it or rather into one of its castes. Rabbinic Judaism, as it developed in the course of history, has completely abandoned the kind of missionary aspiration which had undoubtedly existed for relatively brief periods. No doubt proselytes continued to be accepted as a sort of adoption into the family, but that occurred only in exceptional cases. Not for nothing was the liturgical reading for *Shavuoth* (or Pentecost, the feast of the revelation of the Torah on Mount Sinai and of the conclusion of God's covenant with His people) taken from the book of Ruth, the Moabite proselyte who became the ancestress of the house of David. But that was a long way from saying that the other religions were true and correct. From the Jewish eschatalogical perspective (see Zechariah 14, 9, 'And YHWH will become king over all the earth; on that day YHWH will be one and his name one', in contrast to the more primitive (henotheistic?) Micah 4, 5, 'For all the peoples walk each in the name of its god, but we will walk in the name of YHWH our God for ever and ever'), Christianity, together with its Christology and all its related ideas must, at the end of time when it has finished playing its part as a potential *praeparatio salutis*, simply cease to exist. Similarly in the Christian view, Judaism will perish in the fullness of time and in the fullness of the Kingdom of God – that is to say, of the Kingdom of Christ. To seek to obscure any of this would be irresponsible. So it would be irresponsible to draw on a misinterpretation of Rosenzweig, according to whom allegedly there were only two equally valid religions: Judaism for Israel and Christianity for the rest of mankind, all other religions being false.[1] It would be no less irresponsible to invoke the complementarity of Sinai and Golgotha as it is put forward in the theology of James Parkes. In their eschatologies Judaism and Christianity definitively go in separate ways. This may sound like a deliberately paradoxical *skandalon* but is in fact very simple. In opposition to all those who speak of separate paths supposedly leading to a single eschatological end ('march separately, strike as one'), I offer the view that the eschatologies are indeed irreconcilable but that, precisely because they are eschatologies, the issue can be left to God. It is of decisive importance that Jews and Christians should move together – at least along vital stretches of the road.

What makes this argument relevant is the fact that we are not addressing one another in the *eschaton* but from a pre-eschatological perspective and – which ought to make for even greater urgency as far as we are concerned – in a situation of shared pre-eschatological tribulation and responsibility. It is in this common tribulation and responsibility that we must search for the common root. (I am deliberately and almost programmatically changing my title 'The Common Roots . . .' from the plural to the singular.) The reason is that a revolution has taken place in our generation, the causes and background of which (including the *Shoah*) do not form part of my subject here. Judaism, from Abraham through Moses, David, the Pharisees and the Talmud right down to the present wishes to be regarded as a valid partner *in integrum*, without any renunciation of their Christian beliefs on the part of Christians. My colleague Mussner, among others, has put forward some pertinent thoughts on this matter, even though they still need to be discussed thoroughly by Jews and Christians alike. The reading of his most recent publication, *Die Kraft der Wurzel*, is in fact obligatory for anyone with a serious interest in this problem. In addition to Mussner, I should also like to mention a writer on the Catholic side, Walter Strolz. In the chapter on Christianity and Judaism in his work in three volumes on *Heilswege der Weltreligionen*, Walter Strolz talks more about Talmud, Midrash, Cabbala and Chasidism than about the Old Testament. But Judaism, too, is learning new ways of meeting Christianity, though it still has to overcome much internal and external resistance – *sapienti sat*. Christianity is no longer looked upon as a 'daughter-religion' which was founded by a perhaps great and important Jewish teacher and which then went astray: it is seen as a distinctive religious entity in its own right, which comprises its Christology, its *mysterium trinitatis* (both in the unity of the inner divine life and in the unity of the *opera trinitatis ad extra*), its sacramental doctrine, its sacramental reality and much else besides. But there is another point: the common situation of those who find themselves in a pre-eschatalogical state of tribulation and responsibility requires that Jews attain a better understanding of the Christian belief in the irruption of the eschatology into our pre-eschatological reality and in an already attained salvation within our unsaved and unredeemed world. Here we need to search out what, for all our differences and for all our strangeness to each other, nevertheless links us at the root.

This brings us to the question of that common root. Here we might take an easy conservative line and fall back on the traditional distinction between the religion of the Hebrew Bible and of ancient Israel on the one hand and the – by definition later – religions of Judaism and Christianity on the other. In that case the common root – nothing simpler, as we have already said – would be the so-called Old Testament. However, that is precisely the kind of pseudo-answer I am anxious to avoid, particularly since closer examination might reveal that this root is anything but 'common'. Do Jews and Christians, in contrast with the experts in the exegesis of religious history, who are, of course, entirely objective, really have the same *pagina sacra* before them when they read their *Tanach*, i.e., the Old Testament? Is *how* a person reads not decisive with regard to *what* he reads? Will a person who is reading through Pauline spectacles not read the Old Testament differently from a person who is wearing rabbinic spectacles? What concerns us here is the common root of Christianity *in toto* and of Judaism *in toto*. I stand by this thesis even if it means that I am opening myself to the reproach that I am denying the objectivity of the *pagina sacra* and reading it subjectively. Nevertheless, it is beyond dispute that neither Jews nor Christians, when they talk about a common root, can pass over the *Tanach*/Old Testament. Both must include either the book as a whole or selected parts of it in any discussion of the root.

Before I summarize my principal thesis – in so far as I have one – I should like to illustrate it by an example of this kind of 'selection'. For instance, we might approach our thesis with regard to the idea of the covenant. The covenant is admittedly an Old Testament *theologumenon*, so once again we are forced back to the Hebrew Bible as root. However, I have deliberately chosen this concept because in the past, even if we disregard the no longer entirely fashionable doctrine of substitution, the old covenant has so often and so readily been played off against the new covenant. I should like to set against that the view that there is only one covenant, which is part of the common root. It is neither possible nor permissible to impute a substantive existence to the often hyperbolic metaphors and imagery of the prophets about the new, i.e., the renewed, genuinely re-experienced and fully realized covenant, as envisaged by Jeremiah and others, and grant it an independent existence with clearly polemical intentions. Paul would be incomprehensible to me were I to attribute to him a doctrine of two covenants. Naturally, his interpretation of the events of the covenant and of the fulfilment of the covenant is totally different from that of the Jews who, of course, cannot accept it. Different trees grow from the common root. If we start from the postulate of a single covenant, however, a great deal of the nonsense talked about the difference between the 'oh-so-Jewish' Jesus and the Pauline Christ loses its validity. So does the ostensible 'bringing home' of Jesus to Judaism. Which Jesus: the – Messianic or non-Messianic – sectarian teacher reconstructed by historians, or the Christ acknowledged by the church? And which Judaism: the Judaism of the first century or the developing historical normative Judaism? Jesus himself, in consequence of his eschatological consciousness, had a wholly new understanding of the phases and epochs of the covenant and Torah; it was one in which the pious Jew of the post-Christian era, faithful to the Torah, could not follow him. Paul systematized this understanding of the covenant and the Torah in which the role of the Torah in the history of salvation (to adopt Hartmut Stegemann's terminology) was in fact a 'history of un-salvation' (*Unheilsgeschichte*) which, so Christ proclaimed, could become *Heilsgeschichte* only in the new *aion*. Here the Jewish theologian has no choice, without lapsing into false analogies, but to think of the Cabbalistic doctrine of the entirely different manifestations of the one identical Torah in the pre- and post-Messianic ages.

But discussion of the common root – and let us not call it the Torah or covenant but God – makes sense only if, instead of retrospectively searching for common origins, we look here and now, all divergences and openly acknowledged differences notwithstanding, for shared beliefs and for joint action called forth by these shared beliefs. I am not talking about a united Jewish–Christian front against people of different faiths or so-called atheists. (Who but God knows who the real atheists are?) What interests me is a unique, specific instance of identity within the more general identity of mankind. I am interested in specific identity that has nothing to do with tolerance or the 'dialogue of religions'. Nor am I concerned about a common book (which both as a whole and in its separate parts is capable of being understood in such divisively different ways) but about certain things said in that book, which both Jews and Christians accept as binding. There is God – not only as being (*der Seiende*) but also the ever being-with (*Mitseiende*) and, according to the mystics, also supra-existent (*Überseiende*) – who is also the Creator. What, in a period that until recently was called the post-modern age, do God and Creation mean to Jews and Christians? What is the meaning of the responsibility for Creation that distinguishes man as 'image' of the Creator God from the rest of Creation? And what is this 'Covenant' that binds together human fallibility and divine grace? Will Jews and Christians be able to come together to such an extent that, despite the burdens of the past and of their theological differences, they become inwardly aware of their common root and as a result experience and live out common purposes and a togetherness of the way, of hope (as opposed to optimism), and as witnesses of the certainty of redemption?

These are some of the questions that today's student of religion asks himself when he seeks to understand Judaism and Christianity from within. The response must come from Jews and Christians. Will they continue to be unable to respond, or will they rise up to their responsibility and respond to God when He calls out to each of Adam's descendants: 'Adam, where are you?'

NOTES

[1] Stephen Schwarzschild has shown this to be an erroneous interpretation of Rosenzweig.

II

THE HISTORICAL
BACKGROUND

Jesus the Jew: Christian and Jewish Reactions

GEZA VERMES

In 1956 Professor Günther Bornkamm surprised New Testament scholars by publishing his *Jesus of Nazareth*. In an era dominated, especially in Germany, by Rudolf Bultmann and his school of *Formgeschichte*, professing complete agnosticism towards historical knowledge in the domain of the Gospels, Bornkamm's endeavours must have appeared foolhardy indeed. His nervousness in the face of much potential hostility may account for his opening sentence seemingly contradicting the purpose of his book: 'No one is any longer in the position to write a life of Jesus.'[1]

From another point of view *Jesus of Nazareth* was no novelty at all. It echoed, in fact, as far as Jesus and Judaism were concerned, a very familiar tune. Bornkamm felt constrained to admit that Jesus appears within the Jewish world, but claimed that he unmistakably stands outside it as a stranger[2] because narrow and hardened post-exilic Judaism was a perversion of the Israelite religion.[3] Under the influence of scribes and Pharisees, it developed into a formalistic legalism and a correspondingly 'atomisierende Frömmigkeitstechnik' or 'detailed technique of piety' according to the English edition,[4] a foretaste of Talmudic Judaism against which Jesus stood in sharp contrast.[5]

Although Bornkamm's book is still in print, and in some circles influential, during the last three decades the spirit of the age has greatly changed in regard to Jewish–Christian relations. Thus, for instance, Daniel J. Harrington S.J. chose the Jewishness of Jesus as the subject of his Presidential address in 1986 to the Catholic Biblical Association of America:

The agenda for the Jewish–Christian dialogue is quite full. Starting from our own day, it includes the State of Israel, the Holocaust, Christian persecution of the Jews, the parting of the ways, and so on back to the beginnings of ancient Israel. A major topic on this agenda has been the Jewishness of Jesus.[6]

It seems therefore quite appropriate that an analysis of Jews and Christians in a pluralistic world should also include a study of Jesus the Jew, and investigate contemporary reactions to this cornerstone of any genuine Jewish–Christian dialogue.

But what is meant by the Jewishness of Jesus? And what kind of Jewish and Christian reactions are to be examined?

For the sake of convenience, I will use the comments and criticisms generated, mostly in the English-speaking world, by my two books, *Jesus the Jew*[7] and *Jesus and the World of Judaism*.[8] With the hindsight of fifteen years it is interesting to note that in 1973 the title *Jesus the Jew* was chosen on account of its strength, whereas by now it has more or less become common parlance. 'Jesus was a Jew' was the headline of the Easter leader of *The Times* in 1983, and in the *Observer* of 21 December 1986 Richard Harries, now the Anglican Bishop of Oxford, spoke of 'a continuing (theological) emphasis on Jesus the Jew'. With even greater stress, and under the title 'When Jesus was a Jew', the Reverend Marcus Braybrooke, formerly Executive Director of the British Council for Christians and Jews, opened his article in the *Guardian* of 23 November 1987 as follows: 'That Jesus was a Jew and that his religion was that of a faithful Jew is now widely recognized.' His conclusion is particularly striking: 'Anyone who starts with the historical human being, Jesus of Nazareth, and seeks to understand him in the Jewish milieu of his time, will recognize later Christological developments as mythological. These myths can contain deep insight about the meaning and significance of Jesus, but taken literally they make Jesus the object of worship instead of the Father.'

Jesus the Jew

The greatest Biblical scholar of the last century, Julius Well-hausen, who was hardly a philo-Semite himself – Bornkamm inherited his views on post-exilic Judaism – scandalized his contemporaries by his blunt assertion: 'Jesus was a Jew and not a Christian.'[9] Among those unfamiliar with historical criticism of the Gospels and uninvolved in inter-faith dialogue, Jewish and Christian alike, it still produces shockwaves. Not very long ago, I was taken to task in public for uttering such a scandalous statement by the chaplain to the Roman Catholic students in a British provincial 'red-brick' university. The unenlightened in both camps simply assume that Jesus was a Christian. The more sophisticated Jews, who nevertheless consider 'orthodoxy' an essential constituent of Judaism even prior to the Mishnah, relegate Jesus to the status of a heretic or *min* – an Essene.[10] In contrast, many Christian New Testament scholars would stress and overstress those features of his teaching which conflict with their view of Judaism, and claim that Jesus intended to achieve, according to the title of a recent book, a 'transformation' of Judaism.[11]

Christian experts, even when sympathetic to an approach to Jesus from the Jewish angle, are rarely able to portray him in an apt conceptual context, since they find it impossible to free themselves from the jargon-ridden terminology of Christian theology. The result is often a complete caricature which reminds one of the Talmudic satire in which Moses is transported in spirit to the classroom of Rabbi Akiva, a luminary of the second century CE, renowned for his pernickety interpretation of the Bible. Sitting in the back row, Moses listened as hard as he could, yet failed to grasp the meaning of a single word, let alone realize that the teacher and the pupils were engaged in a discussion of Mosaic law.[12] I think Jesus would be just as flabbergasted if faced by some of the doctrines calmly and automatically attributed to him today.

It is unnecessary to dwell here at length on the religious personality of Jesus, the subject of *Jesus the Jew*. It will suffice to repeat that its principal thesis, based on an examination of first-century Galilean society and religion[13] and an analysis of such titles as Prophet, Lord, Messiah and Son of God given to Jesus in the Synoptic Gospels, is that he was a representative of the miracle-working prophet figure, a latter day manifestation of the type represented by Elijah and Elisha, characterized by me as a charismatic *hasid*.[14] Moreover, he can be shown as belonging to that kind of popular religion excellently sketched some years ago by Professor J.B.Segal.[15] Finally, the miracle-worker-healer-teacher portrait of the earliest Gospel tradition is firmly echoed by the Testimonium Flavianum's idiom of 'wise man' and 'performer of paradoxical deeds', whose authenticity I recently attempted to demonstrate.[16] The postscript of *Jesus the Jew* formulates the same points in less academic phraseology:

What has been the main finding of this exploration of the historical and linguistic elements of which the Gospels are composed? Without doubt, it is that whereas none of the claims and aspirations of Jesus can be said definitely to associate him with the role of Messiah, not to speak of that of *son of man*, the strange creation of modern mythmakers, everything combines ... to place him in the venerable company of the Devout, the ancient Hasidim. Indeed, if the present research has any value at all, it is in this conclusion that it is most likely to reside, since it means that any new enquiry may accept as its point of departure the safe assumption that Jesus did not belong among the Pharisees, Essenes, Zealots or Gnostics, but was one of the holy miracle-workers of Galilee.[17]

On concluding *Jesus the Jew*, I was aware of the danger that readers might take my definition of Jesus as a 'Galilean *hasid*' in a simplistic sense, viz., that he was one of many equals. I was also aware, and if I had not been Professor Henry Chadwick reviewing the book on BBC Radio 3 in March 1974 would have brought it home to me, that no characterization of Jesus is complete without a presentation of his teaching. In fact, in the same postscript, I expressly referred to 'the incomparable superiority of Jesus'. A few years later, for the Riddell Memorial Lectures at the University of Newcastle in 1981, I gave a paper entitled *The Gospel of Jesus the Jew*,[18] a preliminary outline of what appears to be the essential message of the Master from Galilee. I am now developing the same topic further in *The Religion of Jesus and Christianity*.

The purpose of the Riddell Lectures was to sum up the religion preached and practised by Jesus, without any fashionable sociological-exegetical-theological jargon, reconstructing its major traits directly from the Gospels, in the context of inter-Testamental and early rabbinic Judaism. This was performed with the help of some of the proven methods of New Testament criticism, with a refined approach to the ancient Jewish sources, set out subsequently in 'Jewish Literature and New Testament Exegesis: Reflections on Methodology',[19] and definitely with a less negative approach to the problem of the Gospels *qua* historical sources than that characteristic of post-Bultmannian New Testament scholarship.[20]

To turn to the religious teaching of Jesus, we must remember that Jewish masters did not create abstract doctrinal systems, but associated God with the reality they knew.[21] Like the prophets and the sages, Jesus employed an existential language. For him, God was King and Father, both notions being in wide use in his time.

The concept of the Kingdom of God has a long history and it is essential to seek a clear definition of Jesus's own understanding of it. Did he envisage the establishment of the Kingdom of Heaven as a religious-political reality, with himself as the King-Messiah? I doubt it. Jesus does not appear to have planned to challenge the power of Antipas in Galilee, let alone the might of Rome in Judaea. Ed Sanders is to be commended for his pertinent reminder in his book *Jesus and Judaism* that the apostles were not persecuted by Pilate, which surely would have happened if they had been seen as constituting a revolutionary faction.[22] This leaves us with two other concepts of the 'Kingdom'. The first is that of an apocalyptic triumph, with God's rule destroying the ancient realities and replacing them with a new earth and a new heaven. The second sees a holy Jewish nation drawing the Gentile world to God, to the acceptance of the yoke of the Kingdom of Heaven. Jesus's imagery is individual, but is closer to this second idea, to the idea of quiet submission to the divine Ruler. Indeed, the regal imagery mostly vanishes and is replaced by the landscapes, worktools and the people of the Galilean country life. The Kingdom of God is like a field, a vineyard, the mustard seed, the fish, the net, the catch, the woman looking for a lost penny or kneading the dough. The Kingdom of God is entered only by those who, like little children, trust the heavenly Father.

Jesus paid no attention to the precise moment when the Kingdom was to arrive. He did not imitate the author of Daniel and speculate on the seventy weeks of years or foreshadow St Paul with his detailed schedule of the rebellion, the arrival of the man of lawlessness, his enthronement in the Temple, his destruction by the Lord Jesus, and finally the dawning of the Day (2 Thess. 2, 3–8). According to Jesus, there will be no premonitory signs. God alone knows the hour. He entered the final age in a spirit of faith. When the call of John the Baptist moved him to repentance, he and those who obeyed with him the call to turning, to *Teshuvah*, made their decisive choice. As a result, they found themselves in God's Kingdom.

Unlike his Jewish contemporaries, Jesus did not address God as King; he called him Father. This divine name figures in the Bible and the Apocrypha, very seldom in the Dead Sea Scrolls, but frequently in the synagogical prayers with their 'our Father, our King'. According to the Mishnah, the ancient *hasidim* spent a full hour in concentration 'in order to direct their hearts towards their Father who is in heaven'. Jesus appears to have mostly used the short invocation 'Father', the Aramaic 'Abba', signifying 'Father' or 'My Father'. It could be applied in both human and divine contexts. A Talmudic play on words tells of Abba Hanan, a late first-century BC charismatic, who during a severe drought was followed by children in the street, shouting, 'Abba, Abba, give us rain!' Hearing them, he begged God to 'render service to those who cannot distinguish the Abba who gives rain from the Abba who does not'. Abba is a dignified and respectful appellation and not, as Joachim Jeremias claimed, a small child's address to his father.[23] The title of a very learned paper by Professor James Barr appears to settle the matter: *Abba isn't 'Daddy'*.[24]

The teaching of Jesus on the Fatherhood of God appears most clearly in the Lord's Prayer where he appeals to him as 'Father', and following the pattern of the famous Jewish prayer, the Kaddish, asks for the sanctification of his name and the establishment of his sovereignty. In the second half of the prayer, Jesus entreats God to exercise his fatherly care, forgiveness and protection. Not that he was not aware that all was not perfect in this world. Then as now, fledglings fell from the nest, little ones perished and the righteous suffered injustice. But Jesus was not a propounder of syntheses: he set out, instead, to *do* his Father's will and enjoined his disciples to devote themselves to the same task, irrespective of its outcome.

Having sketched Jesus's vision of the deity, let us try to discern his religion.

To begin with, he lived in a world where private and public existence – work, business, property, clothing, food, sex – was regulated by the Torah, the Law of Moses. Since Jesus is nowhere said to have failed to pay his debts, beaten up his opponents or committed adultery, he may be presumed to have accepted, respected and observed the common laws and customs in force among his compatriots.

He also depicted as obedient to religious commandments, attending the synagogue on the sabbath, journeying to Jerusalem and visiting the Temple, and celebrating the Passover. Like his elder contemporary, the philosopher Philo, he saw the Ten Commandments as the summary of all other laws. Like Talmudic rabbis, he sought to reduce the many precepts to the double commandment of love of God and men. Like

Hillel, and others, he adopted a single, simple and practical rule, 'Whatever you wish that people do to you, do so to them!', as incorporating the whole of the Law and the Prophets. In the wording of Luke, a Greek addressing Greeks, he declared that 'It is easier for heaven and earth to pass away than for a tittle of the Law to fall'. Luke's statement is absolute: in the divinely predetermined world order, the disintegration of the cosmos is less difficult to envisage than the loss of a single 'tittle' of the Law. Since apart from Judaeo-Christianity, to which Luke certainly did not belong, no branch of the primitive church could conceivably have welcomed a straight assertion of the permanency of the Law, it is truly astonishing that the saying has survived in its blunt simplicity.

Of course, we know that some sayings of Jesus, mainly concerning dietary rules and healing on the sabbath, are presented as clashing with the Law. To judge these matters, it must be borne in mind that Galileans are often portrayed as inexpert in legal matters or holding views different from those in force in Judaea.[25] But more importantly, Jesus lived in an age prior to the unification of the legal teachings of Judaism, before the (attempted) imposition of an 'orthodoxy' by rabbis of the second century CE. As for his alleged abrogation of *kashrut*, of the dietary regulations, this would be difficult to reconcile with the continued observance of food laws by his Palestinian disciples. Remember the famous conflict in Antioch between Paul and Peter in connection with the latter's rejection of table-companionship with Gentile converts because of the presence of 'Judaizing' Palestinian Christians. Surely such a situation would not have arisen if Jesus had positively liberalized his own and his disciples' eating habits.

Moreover, Jesus is depicted as urging express obedience to cultic laws relating to the purification of lepers, the observance of tithing and the sending of donations to the Temple.[26] He is even described, with poker-faced humour, as willing to contribute to the upkeep of the Jerusalem Sanctuary. The first fish Peter would catch would hold in its mouth a shekel coin, sufficient for both himself and Jesus to pay their annual instalment of the Temple tax.

The true distinguishing mark of Jesus's piety lies in his emphasis on the inner religious significance of the Commandments. True, the Qumran sectaries and the rabbis also insisted on inwardness and sincerity. But in the eschatological perspective of Jesus, interiority and purity of intention were bound to gain a dominating position. He stressed the primary causes and the ultimate purpose of moral or immoral acts: anger leading to murder, lustful thought to adultery.[27] Likewise almsgiving, prayer, fasting are to be performed before God alone and not for the sake of being admired by men.

In brief, the religious deed of Jesus obtained its special effectiveness through his grasp of the Torah's original intention, namely that it should serve as a vehicle for an authentic relation of a child to his Father, permeated by simplicity and confidence, the Hebrew virtue of *emunah*. It demands that God's children should lay aside material anxieties and commit themselves unreservedly to his care. It demands also single-minded devotion and prompt action. No delay is tolerated. No room is left for bargaining. He who has found a treasure in a field, must rush and sell all he possesses and buy that field at once.

In the religion of Jesus, one principle stands out: that of the imitation of God, a well-attested Jewish doctrine. It is the divine attribute of mercy that provides the ultimate model for action. 'Be merciful as your Father is merciful.' But this mercy and love towards others must be pure, hoping for no repayment. Using rhetorical exaggeration to hammer home his teaching, Jesus chooses the unrealistic case of the love of enemies to insinuate the nature and conditions of genuine love. 'If you love those who do good to you, what credit is that to you? . . . But love your enemies . . . expecting nothing in return . . . and you will be sons of the Most High.' By becoming the 'friend of tax-collectors and sinners', Jesus was imitating in his own life the conduct of the heavenly Father towards those of his wayward children whose turning causes more joy in Heaven (another overstatement?) than the habitual virtue of ninety-nine just.

Such is the outline of the religion taught and practised by Jesus the Jew, a God-centred real religion enacted by a God-loving real man. But this religion was soon, within a century after Golgotha, replaced in the Christian church by one in which at the side of the heavenly Father a redeeming divine Christ acquires an ever-increasing role, the great worshipper of God himself becoming the (central?) object of worship. This statement, which is not a hyperbole, concludes my sketch of Jesus the Jew and we turn now to Christian and Jewish reactions to it.

Christian and Jewish Reactions

After the publication of *Jesus the Jew* in 1973, I expected a barrage of criticism, both Jewish and Christian. To my great surprise, this did not materialize. There have, of course, been scholarly disagreements, but since I am concerned here not with academic argument, but with more deep-seated reactions, only those prompted by religious attitudes will be taken into account.

On the Jewish side, there seems to have been some initial nervousness. The subject must have been thought by some to be dangerous. This may explain why both the influential London *Jewish Chronicle* and *Judaism* in the United States assigned *Jesus the Jew* to Christian reviewers.[28] Cautious Jewish criticism was focused partly on the book's assertion that a scholarly-critical reading of the Gospels does not point to Jesus's awareness, let alone self-proclamation, of being the Messiah,[29] but mostly on the description of Jesus – in the postscript of *Jesus the Jew* – as 'second to none in profundity of insight and grandeur of character' and as 'an unsurpassed master of the art of laying bare the innermost core of spiritual truth'.[30] This was thought to be an overstatement.

In Christian ranks, there have been public outbursts on

a few occasions. What happened behind closed doors is impossible to know, although rumour has it that Desclée, the Catholic publishers of the French *Jésus le Juif*, were severely reprimanded in private by irate bishops. An outraged female contributor to the extreme right-wing publication *La pensée catholique* reacted to the book as blasphemous scandal.[31] Intermittently, even scholars in the United States have expressed their bad temper openly. One, a Protestant New Testament expert, concludes: 'Jesus the Jew deserves better than this.'[32] Another, a Jesuit professor, remarked: 'I am always immediately put off by those who claim to write about the gospels as "historians"; that immediately means that an axe is being ground.'[33] But these are exceptions. The majority of the reviewers seem to find in this 'historian's approach' worthwhile openings for a fuller understanding of the real Jesus and, on the Christian side, a firmer basis for theology and belief.

Jewish reactions, perhaps for understandable reasons – Jesus is not indispensable for an understanding of Judaism – are sporadic, but generally hopeful. Thus David Daube, the renowned author of *The New Testament and Rabbinic Judaism* (1956), concludes his review of *Jesus the Jew*: 'Whether it will do much towards removing ill-will and distrust may be doubted. These attitudes are largely independent of scholarly data. Still, with luck, it may do a little. The present climate gives some ground for hope.'[34] David Flusser, of the Hebrew University, himself an author on Jesus, is equally positive in his forecast.[35] Also, a few years ago, in its issue of 7 December 1984, the *Jerusalem Post* carried an article by Magen Broshi, Director of the Shrine of the Book where the Dead Sea Scrolls are housed, presenting *Jesus the Jew* as the ideal book for Jews 'who know little or nothing about Jesus', and who when told that he was a Jew, would think that their leg is being pulled. 'Actually,' Broshi remarks, 'Jesus was so Jewish that a modern (Israeli) reader of the Gospels might even find some of his anti-Gentile utterances somewhat embarrassing.'

The presentation of a genuinely Jewish portrayal of Jesus has also earned a fair number of constructive Christian appraisals.[36] Starting from the evangelical wing of Protestantism, a lecturer at the London Bible College amicably warns his readers: 'You may find it [the book] sometimes fascinating, sometimes infuriating, but generally a salutary challenge to re-examine your historical perspective on Jesus the Jew.'[37] And again, Professor F.F.Bruce firmly states: 'I can do no other than read the contents of this volume through the eyes of a New Testament student. As I do so, one message comes through loud and clear: no one can understand or expound the New Testament adequately without an acquaintance with Jewish thought and life of the relevant period.'[38]

More towards the centre of the British Protestant spectrum, Professor J.L.Houlden lists 'a number of truths, some of them uncongenial, most of them neglected by reason of prejudice or inertia' which *Jesus and the World of Judaism* stresses. At the same time, this writer adds, Jesus is not merely merged into his Jewish setting. He is in no way de-personalized, and his special voice is appreciated. All this is presented with general approval, although it is suggested, to its author's disappointment, that the study sometimes fails in lucidity.[39] Another positive assessment, followed by qualifications, was produced by Anthony Harvey, now Canon of Westminster, formerly a Fellow, like myself, of Wolfson College, Oxford:

The more you stress the Jewishness of Jesus, the harder you make it to understand that extraordinarily un-Jewish ability of his to cut a figure, and propound a message, which has had a profound influence on so many nations throughout the world – except the Jews.[40]

On the Roman Catholic side, Nicholas King S.J., after referring to 'easy sympathy with the two overlapping worlds of Judaism and Christianity', and to a 'delight in questioning all established orthodoxies within both Jewish and Christian scholarship', concludes: 'We can learn in the process how closely the two partners of Judaeo-Christianity belong together, and how much we depend on each other.'[41]

So far I have attempted to trace on the individual level the movement that has been taking place during the last dozen years or so in Jewish and Christian circles in regard to Jesus the Jew. It should be noted, at this juncture, that an individual scholar, even when firmly attached to an organized religious body, can afford himself a relatively large amount of freedom in expressing his opinion on a delicate subject. After all, his scholarly reputation alone is at stake and he is responsible ultimately to his conscience only.

By contrast, when it comes to hazarding views on the same subjects in the context of inter-faith consultations, official representatives of churches and Jewish organizations as a rule display little willingness to touch on dangerous topics. None of the fifteen papers included in the recently published *Fifteen Years of Catholic–Jewish Dialogue: 1970–1985* by the International Catholic–Jewish Liaison Committee (1988) venture into a controversially constructive area.[42] As for the Anglican–Jewish consultations planned for 1986 on the subject of Jesus, with academic specialists recruited to represent both sides, they were at the last minute cancelled on the insistence of one of the authorities, and subsequently replaced by a joint discussion of the problem of the inner city!

However, there are two recent exceptions to the rule that in the domain of Judaeo-Christian dialogue the views of the other party are given a favourable evaluation by an official body. The first of them was established in 1983 by the Roman Catholic church. Its Pontifical Biblical Commission, a learned committee of Biblical exegetes, accorded a reasonably positive role to contemporary Jewish scholarship in an official statement on *Scripture and Christology*.[43]

After the First World War, some Jewish historians, abandoning a centuries-old animosity – of which Christian preachers were themselves not innocent – devoted studies directly to Jesus and to Christian origins (J.Klausner, M.Buber, J.[*sic*, instead of C.]G.Montefiore, etc.)... Certain borrowings were investigated ... in Qumran literature by Jewish historians (Y.Yadin, etc.) ... Some Jewish historians, turning their interest and attention to 'brother Jesus' (S.Ben Chorin), have set in relief certain lines of his personality; they have found in him a teacher like the Pharisees of old (D.Flusser) or a wonder-worker similar to those whose memory Jewish tradition has preserved (G.Vermes). Some have not hesitated to compare the passion of Jesus with the Suffering Servant, mentioned in the Book of Isaiah (M.Buber). All these attempts (at interpretation) are to be accorded serious attention by Christian theologians engaged in the study of Christology ...[44] This is the basis on which a fruitful dialogue between Jews and Christians can be initiated.[45]

As may be surmised, limits are later set on the usefulness of such studies, for if conducted only along such lines, 'there is always danger of mutilating his [Jesus's] personality'.[46] But in a document of this type, such comments are unavoidable. All the same, I believe that *Scripture and Christology* constitutes a major breakthrough, an official Christian recognition of the value, and to some extent even the necessity, of Jewish studies for an improved Christian theology. The same basic idea underlies Resolution 21 on 'Inter-faith Dialogue' agreed by the Lambeth Conference of the Anglican Communion in 1988.[47]

Clearly, this type of declaration cannot be expected from Jews, since Judaism has no authoritative institution similar to the Pontifical Biblical Commission. However, when a scholar of such unimpeachable orthodoxy as Professor Shmuel Safrai of the Hebrew University, writing in 1985 on the ancient *hasidim*, explicitly lists Jesus of Nazareth as one of them, although in an article on the same subject published twenty years earlier he totally ignored him,[48] we realize that a whisper, if not a wind, of change is blowing even in traditional Jewish circles.

Outstanding Questions

The recent re-awakening of interest in the quest for the historical Jesus, initiated by Albert Schweitzer some eighty years ago, relinquished as hopeless in the wake of the passing triumph of Rudolf Bultmann's *Formgeschichte* school, but revived again during the last twenty or twenty-five years in the form of a search for the Jewish Jesus, raises important and difficult questions of three kinds.

First the academic, with or without religious commitments, will continue to face the challenge of the scarcity and limited reliability of the evidence out of which he has to reconstruct the life, personality and message of an historical figure. Two questions are likely to haunt him in all the foreseeable future: How can non-historical sources yield historical data? Can rabbinic literature of a somewhat later vintage be used for the study of first century AD Judaism?

Secondly, these problems, attached in one way or another to traditional Judaism, are confronted by a different set of questions. Today, Judaism and Christianity are two distinct entities, but possess in common centuries of hostility culminating in the Holocaust. Was Jesus himself responsible for the break between the synagogue and the church and for the anti-Jewish tendencies in Christianity? If not, what should be the Jewish attitude to him? Does he deserve, as Martin Buber suggested, 'a great place in Israel's history of faith'?[49] And if so, what has he to offer to Judaism and what should Jews do about it?

Finally, these sensitive and highly emotional Jewish issues are nevertheless insignificant compared with the questions awaiting Christian answers. For if the religion preached and practised by Jesus even roughly resembles the picture outlined in this paper, it surely does not reflect, but rather clashes with, traditional, dogmatic, Christocentric, Trinitarian Christianity. And if historic Christianity is not the religion of Jesus the Jew, nor the religion taught by him, can a Christian departure from it be justified? If not, what should Christians do?

NOTES

[1] *Jesus von Nazareth*, Stuttgart, 1956. [English translation: *Jesus of Nazareth*, London, 1960].
[2] 'Ein unverwechselbar anderer', ibid., p. 51.

[3] Ibid., p. 33.
[4] Ibid., p. 40. 'Atomisierende Frömmigkeitstechnik' in the German original.
[5] Ibid., pp. 36–7.
[6] *Catholic Biblical Quarterly* 49 (1987), p. 1.
[7] Henceforward *JJ*, London, 1981; Philadelphia, 1986. It is also available in French, Spanish and Italian translations: *Jésus le Juif*, Paris, 1978; *Jesús el Judío*, Barcelona, 1977; *Gesú l'Ebreo*, Rome, 1983.
[8] Henceforward *JWJ*, London, 1983; Philadelphia, 1984.
[9] Quoted in *JWJ*, pp. 147, n. 17; 169, n. 1.
[10] *Who was Jesus?*, Lanham, 1986.
[11] *Jesus and the Transformation of Judaism*, London, 1980.
[12] Babylonian Talmud *Menahoth* 29b.
[13] The Galilean setting of the charismatic religious phenomenon, reflected by the activity of Jesus, has been argued also by S. Safrai in 'Hassidim and Men of Deeds', *Zion* 50 (1985), pp. 133–54, esp. p. 137.
[14] The notion of charismatic authority was first developed by Max Weber in his posthumously published *Wirtschaft und Gesellschaft* (1921), pp. 753–7; see *Max Weber: Essays in Sociology*, translated and edited by H. H. Gerth and C. Wright Mills, 1979, pp. 245–64. See also D. L. Tiede, *The Charismatic Figure as Miracle Worker*, 1973. For the categorization of Jesus as a charismatic, see Rudolf Otto, *The Kingdom of God and the Son of Man*, London, 1943, pp. 333–76. See also Irving M. Zeitlin, *Jesus and the Judaism of his Time*, 1988.
[15] 'Popular Religion in Ancient Israel', *Journal of Jewish Studies* (henceforward *JJS*) 27 (1976), pp. 1–22.
[16] 'The Jesus-Notice of Josephus Reconsidered', *JJS* 38 (1987), pp. 1–10.
[17] *JJ*, p. 223.
[18] Newcastle-upon-Tyne, 1981.
[19] *JWJ*, pp. 74–88, 173–5.
[20] 'The reaction of some recent scholars against the extreme uncertainty expressed by many form critics is probably justified: whatever the problems in reconstructing the life and career of Jesus (and they are immense), it is more plausible than otherwise that the general outline of his career as presented in the Gospel biographies is correct, simply because the hypothesis that these accounts were entirely composed, rather than partially altered, to make a theological point is more implausible than the belief that the outlines of Jesus's career are correctly described; among other objections to the former (and commonly held) view are the survival within each Gospel of contradictory views of Jesus and oddness of biography as a vehicle for theological didacticism.' (M. Goodman, *The Ruling Class of Judaea*, Cambridge, 1987, pp. 22–3.)

21 For a fuller version of this section, see *JWJ*, pp. 30–57.

22 *Jesus and Judaism*, London, 1985, pp. 301–2.

23 *The Prayers of Jesus*, London, 1977, pp. 57–62.

24 *Journal of Theological Studies* 39 (1988), pp. 28–47.

25 Valuable light will be thrown on this subject in a forthcoming essay by Martin D.Goodman in *The Cambridge History of Judaism*.

26 The thesis advanced by some New Testament scholars of a re-Judaization by Matthew of an un-Jewish Mark (and Jesus) goes against the current of the evolution of early Christian thought. The latter rather tends to obliterate the typically Jewish elements in the teaching of Jesus in favour of a universal formulation of his message.

27 Far from 'shattering the letter of the Law', as E.Käsemann insensitively suggested (*Essays on New Testament Themes*, London, 1964, p. 37ff), the so-called 'antitheses' reveal the depth of the Torah and seek to reinforce it. When, after quoting 'Thou shalt not kill!', he (or the evangelist interpreting him) adds, 'but I say to you', the 'antithesis' enjoins, not that homicide is permissible, let alone obligatory, but that the likelihood of murder should be preempted by outlawing anger, leading to verbal insult and possibly to physical violence.

28 J.W.Parkes and G.S.Sloyan.

29 See for example D.Daube in *JJS* 25 (1974), p. 334.

30 *JJ*, p. 224.

31 D.J. in *La pensée catholique* 176 (1978), p. 88.

32 *JBL* 95 (1975), p. 509.

33 *Journal for the Study of the New Testament* 4 (1979), p. 67, n. 33.

34 *JJS* 25 (1974), p. 336.

35 'Jesus and the World of Judaism', *Judaism* 35 (1986), pp. 361–4.

36 See the late G.Lindeskog's posthumously published excellent study, *Das jüdisch–christliche Problem. Randglossen zu einer Forschungsepoche*, Stockholm, 1986. The same scholar's doctoral dissertation appeared in 1938 under the title, *Die Jesusfrage im neuzeitlichen Judentum*.

37 *Themelios*, April 1985, pp. 29–30. See also D.A.Hasgner's *The Jewish Reclamation of Jesus: An Analysis and Critique of Modern Jewish Study of Jesus*, Grand Rapids, Zondervan, 1984. In his preface, the author bluntly states: 'The Jewish reclamation of Jesus has been possible only by being unfair to the Gospels', p. 14.

38 *JJS* 35 (1984), p. 106.

39 *Religious Studies* 21 (1984), pp. 107–8.

40 *The Times Literary Supplement*, February 24, 1984, p. 199.

41 *The Heythrop Journal*, 1986, pp. 202–3.

42 The only paper, delivered in Madrid in 1978, touching the question of Jewish attitudes to Jesus is a non-committal, and not fully up-to-date, historical survey by the late S.B.Hoenig, formerly of Yeshiva University,

New York, 'A Survey of Jewish Scholarship through the Ages on Jesus and Christianity', pp. 87–102.

[43] J.A.Fitzmyer, *Scripture and Christology: A Statement of the Biblical Commission with a Commentary*, London, 1986.

[44] The Commission's advice was anticipated in what strikes one as the most unlikely context by J.P.Mackey in *The Christian Experience of God as Trinity*, London, 1983.

[45] Ibid., pp. 9–10.

[46] Ibid., p. 23.

[47] 'Modern biblical scholarship is increasingly becoming a joint enterprise between Jews and Christians. Recent Jewish research has shed much light on the complex and varied religious and social situation in Palestine during the first century of the Common Era ... *Some Jews have become very aware of Jesus as part of their own history, and their writings have brought home to Christians his Jewishness* [my emphasis]. Renewed study of Jewish sources by Christian scholars has led them to see first-century Judaism in a new and more positive light ... The New Testament picture of Judaism needs to be supplemented by expressions of faith by Jews of the time if first-century Judaism is to be properly understood.' (Text of the unpublished resolution kindly supplied by the Right Reverend Richard Harries, Bishop of Oxford.)

[48] See article *cit.* in n. 8 above, and 'The Teaching of Pietists in Mishnaic Literature', *JJS* 16 (1965), pp. 15–33.

[49] M.Buber, *Two Types of Faith*, New York, 1961, p. 13.

How Jews and Christians Saw Each Other in the West and in East Central Europe in Pre-modern Times

ALEKSANDER GIEYSZTOR

Perception and feeling, perception and imagination, and their intellectual, social and emotional motivation belong to the domain of any history that aspires to completeness. In them the historian finds an imaginary realm of social realities reduced to stereotyped formulae, the product of repetitive associations of various ideas, symbols and other phenomena. Such formulae, rooted in different social strata, are handed down through the tradition that guides social awareness. Very often simplistic and enshrined in myth, usually irrational in their defence of social practices, they weigh heavily. They also outlive the realities of the time. Around 1500 Western Europe – England in particular – sadly found itself *judenrein*, or virtually so, yet the stereotyped image of the Jew, Shakespeare's Shylock, persisted.

The legacy of antiquity was a triple perspective of relations – experienced and transferred to the theoretical plane – between Jews, pagans and Christians. In Christian apologetics this division of mankind helped the tribe of Christ to distinguish itself from that of Abraham. On the other hand the steadfast loyalty of the Jews of the diaspora to their faith, doctrine and customs confirmed their religious and cultural identity. The fourth century saw Christianity converted to the world before the world had become converted to Christianity. The last pagan intellectuals made their exit advocating religious toleration and a peaceful mutual acceptance by all faiths, Christianity included. Their place in Christian writings was to be taken up by the heretics, while the same apologetics combined with imperial legislation to oppose any form of Jewish proselytism. From that time onwards the Jews, as the only people outside the Christian community, had to face the theological aversion of Christian intellectuals. Isolated from other religious minorities as well, hard hit by the law and by the politics of power, the Jews had to deal alone with constant, impersonal repetition of the stereotype of *perfidia Iudaeorum*, an expression covering those who did not profess true religion, who were in fact traitors to it, and who were dangerous and harmful even without appearing to be so.

However, in the Western world, Jews and Christians lived through the High Middle Ages as tolerable neighbours, sometimes even as good neighbours. An exception was the seventh-century Spanish drama of the mass forced conversions of Jews promulgated by the Visigothic kings. (Arab rule was to bring them full toleration.) Elsewhere the Western empire broke up into separate kingdoms peopled by tribes and ethnic groups. Many and various, these gave rise to the principle and the practice of national, even private law. The Jewish law did not acquire the character of such a law because for a long time the Jews continued to count as Romans. As Roman law disappeared, they gradually came under the special protection of the secular power. Nevertheless, at no time and in no place was the Jewish religion called into question. Despite occasional local and temporary vexations and restrictions, it continued to be allowed along with its laws, rites and ceremonies, places of worship, and religious books and objects. The Jews' pronounced sense of identity served them well, particularly as regards internal use within their communities. Outwardly, they submitted to the common law.

Jews spoke the same language as the Christians around them, keeping their knowledge of Hebrew for religious and cultural use. The rabbinic authorities even appear to have allowed translation into the vulgar tongue during Bible readings and prayers in order to render them fully intelligible to the congregation. Jews practised the same trades and professions as merchants, doctors, farmers, sailors and others. Up until the twelfth century no occupation could be regarded as specifically Jewish, although the international trading network created and run by Jews impressed contemporary witnesses. Jews also lived in the same houses as Christians. We have to wait until the tenth century for the first mention of a Jewish quarter; it was a spontaneous and in no way coercive living arrangement typical for the Rhineland towns up until the twelfth century. And Jews dressed in the same way as other townsfolk. It was not until the twelfth century that iconography began to stress their distinctive outward appearance.

During this period of relatively peaceful coexistence, punctuated by local clashes and patches of friction, the mutual perceptions of Jews and Christians were governed by a particular perspective, that of missionary competition. On the Christian side, that mission employed methods ranging from persuasion and prayer through offers of material advantages and prestige all the way to the use of force. On the Jewish side, proselytism was a matter of the occasional individual being attracted by the Mosaic religion at the intellectual and moral level. Examples of such conversions were Bodo, deacon to Charlemagne's son Louis the Pious, Archbishop Andrew of Bari and John of Oppido–Obadiah in the last quarter of the eleventh century, all of whom were obliged to go into exile. There were also humble converts won on an individual basis, servants and slaves who adopted the Jewish faith and were welcomed into Jewish communities. We have no knowledge of the numbers involved, but the vigilance of the church in this regard is surely significant. Anti-Jewish measures were aimed at preventing the recruitment of followers of the Jewish religion and opposing all contacts regarded as too close, which nevertheless gave rise to influences of a more or less permanent and visible nature. Traces can be detected on the Jewish side in rites (though these are debatable), in the commemoration of souls, in the Yom Kippur great pardon, in the Avodah genuflexion, in synagogue architecture and in Jewish folklore, all very quickly assimilated. On the Christian side, there were fears at the beginning of the Middle Ages that orthodoxy was threatened by such syncretic phenomena as not working on the sabbath and by various forms of Judaizing heresy based on Old Testament exegesis and on certain Jewish customs (sabbath fasting, dietary precepts).

All these relationships left intact the hold that the two religions exercised over their followers. Belief and ritual separated the two communities. However, living together in the same place led to a mutual curiosity. Sometimes Jews even attended Christian services, to which they were welcomed by preachers who vainly attempted to convert them. Theological discussions occupied writers on both sides, who saw them as an aid to affirmation and as a method of proselytism. Christian intellectuals entered into them, drawing their information directly from Jews, as did the Carolingian scholar Rabanus Maurus, who in his interpretations of Scripture referred to a *Hebraeus moderni temporis*. If they wished to learn Hebrew and to get to know the Hebraic writings, this was the only way of doing so. Genuine debates took place as late as the 1030s. The place was Regensburg, the subject was miraculous healing and the parties were the monks of St Emmeram and the Jews of the town. Peter Damian believed in the usefulness of these discussions for bringing about conversions. Towards the end of the eleventh century there was an animated dialogue at Westminster between the abbot, Gilbert Crispin, and a Jew from Mainz in the context of business relations that turned into mutual esteem and gave rise to religious discussions. The Jewish participants in these conversations had a good knowledge of the New Testament, of Christian thought and of the religious life of the church. The Christian arguments served as the basis for a rich polemical literature. That literature had Jewish voices taking up traditional subjects of convention – Christian image worship, the veneration of saints, belief in miracles – but also preaching the coming of the Messiah who would set his people free. We possess only fragments of the Latin writings representing the work of the converted deacon, Bodo, and of Vecolin, a scholar who embraced Judaism around 1006. They drew their inspiration from an intransigent monotheism. Hebrew writings included a parody of the Gospels, *Toledoth Yeshu*, that dated from the early Christian period but was recycled in Medieval times in such a way as to present Christianity as a distortion of true religion and Jesus in terms that, to Christians, were blasphemous in the extreme.

All these things went on in an atmosphere in which demonstrations of hostility, sporadic flare-ups, and anti-Jewish riots certainly occurred, but it is hardly possible to speak of a generalized, harmful feeling of resentment. Certain local campaigns by the church beyond the Pyrenees and in Spain to force Jews to accept baptism were not taken up by the secular rulers. In other words, the Christian world remained fairly tolerant of the Jewish religion so long as that religion did not persuade Christians to join its ranks.

This tolerance, albeit relative, forms a welcome contrast to the sombre prospect of the centuries to come. Protected by the prince's law, living in virtually self-governing communities, Jews were not in principle allowed to have Christian servants. They were barred – officially at least – from holding public office and from plying certain trades, notably those having to do with food. All sexual contact between Jews and Christians was forbidden, and Jews were excluded from military service. They were still present in agriculture, the craft trades and commerce, but in the eleventh century Jewish involvement in the latter was more local than formerly and tended to be concentrated in financial services (short-term loans against security). Though convenient for princes and noblemen, their activities in this field attracted the reprobation of the church and the antipathy of debtors, who lost no time in seizing an opportunity to cancel their debts.

It was at a key stage in history that Abelard wrote his

Dialogus inter philosophum, Iudaeum et Christianum, a dream vision that was hardly conclusive even as far as the author himself was concerned. During an imaginary debate the first participant, a monotheistic philosopher, possibly from one of the Muslim countries, sets out to defend the law of reason and nature by demonstrating the contradictions implicit in a literal understanding of the law as practised by the two representatives of the *fidei sectae*, the Jew and the Christian. Oddly, it was around the same time that Rabbi Yehuddah Halevi of Tudela wrote his apologetic treatise in the form of a discussion among four persons: a Christian philosopher, a Muslim, a Jew and a Khazar – who is in fact converted to Judaism at the end of the argument. Abelard's dialogue applies logic to theological exposition. The uncommitted philosopher is favourable to Christianity; the Jew – an Old Testament expert – is inclined to acknowledge the truth of both laws, the Old and the New; and the Christian accepts the partial truths of his partners in order to reinforce his own truth, his faith in Christ.

The beginnings of a change in this attitude, which when all is said and done was fairly respectful of the liberty of the individual, became apparent during the eleventh century. Although the early years of the century saw expulsions of Jews from a few towns in Germany and France and some forced baptisms, such phenomena remained without sequel. Before long, however, the accusation of treason because of their understanding with the Muslims began to weigh heavily on the Jews, and the fateful subject of the Christicide reared its head once more. In Toulouse it was to give rise to a shameful custom: every Eastertide a Jew had to be publicly slapped in the face by a Christian in a kind of ritual act of vengeance for the death of the Christ. A rash of anti-Jewish and anti-pagan texts from late antiquity – including some Augustinian and pseudo-Augustinian writings – re-emerged and were copied, commented on and propagated. The resumption of the tripartite perception of mankind – Christians, Jews, and Muslims taking the place of the pagans – furnished intellectual landmarks for grasping certain convergences but to an even greater extent fundamental differences that could not be smoothed away.

How did it start, one wonders – this slow but inexorable change? How were populations that had hitherto been peaceful both in principle and in daily practice able to become intolerant and violent towards the Jewish people? We agree with those who seek the causes of this dramatic turnaround in the development of European society. In the deep disarray of the early feudal age, that society was trying both to strengthen the institutions of the old order and at the same time to create new forms of social organization. Before or almost before the latter emerged, Christianity was itself to undergo a renewal. A shifting religious sensibility found a fresh blossoming centred more on the interiorization of faith than on performance of the rituals of Christian magic and observance of a legal morality. From the eleventh century onwards the New Testament – particularly St Matthew's Gospel and the Acts of the Apostles – gave direct nourishment to Christian souls. Christ the redeemer, salvation and the cross appeared at the centre of religious life. This Christocentric devotion also drew sustenance from the apostolic life as a universal model. Then in the twelfth century there was a fresh emphasis on Marian devotion and on the worship of the saints. On the other hand, this evangelical revival actually led men to doubt authority, both ecclesiastical and secular, that doubt finding expression in certain heresies that became popular cults. The papacy and various strands of monastic reform sought for their part to reorganize the Christian universality of the West in a renewal of piety and a period of rapid expansion in many spheres of human life.

Western society was undergoing some very profound changes as the eleventh century gave way to the twelfth. It was becoming aware of its Christian identity over against the other monotheistic religions that were seen as threatening it. The period when Christians had frequented synagogues and welcomed interested Jews into their churches was over, never to return. Studies have been made of works of art, notably of the iconography of the synagogue *vis-à-vis* the church. Prior to the twelfth century, Christian sculptors represented the synagogue as an expression of proud, contemptuous rebellion. After the twelfth century it becomes blind, with eyes bandaged, spear broken and the Tablets of the Law slipping from its grasp – a symbol of poverty, failure, defeat and degradation.

The outcome of an earlier, little-known development, this transformation had its origins in the deepening evangelization of the rural areas that supplied the populations of the developing towns and cities. Catholic Christian society, as structured by the church but also in its spontaneous forms, began to oppose everything outside itself: recalcitrant heretics, Muslims, Slav and Baltic pagans. And it began to adopt a hostile attitude towards the Jews, whose place in society was henceforth dictated by an endless series of interdicts sanctioned by a burgeoning canon law.

The first region to follow the crusading call was southern France, the earliest affected by these new forms of religious expression. When Urban II issued his appeal and the princes responded by mounting expeditions in 1095–6, there were no massacres of the Jewish population, though Jews were numerous in the region. In the Germanic countries of the north, on the other hand, the crusade split into armies of knights and popular movements that defied all forms of authority. The Jews, though fewer in number, found themselves the victims of an explosion of bloodthirsty hatred on the part of a popular group of crusaders for which the contingents of knights and barons, even including Peter the Hermit and the masses that followed his banner, shared none of the responsibility. No more did Emperor Henry IV and the bishops, who opposed these crimes. Up until the capture of Jerusalem the troops of knights made no attacks on Jews.

What, then, was represented by this menacing group led by a minor count, Emicho von Leiningen? Religious sociology has an answer. The religiosity of the individuals who constituted it was that of the lowest stratum of the population. It was based on extremely primitive beliefs: a billy goat and a goose inspired by the Holy Spirit were to guide Emicho to the Holy Land. This was a degraded form of religiosity, in other words – as degraded as the place that such dropouts occupied in society. The crusade gave them a rallying-cry. Under the sign of the cross, which they were simply using, they indulged in savage mass killings of the Jews of Cologne, Mainz, Worms and other towns along their route. Disoriented by their own religious fervour, still believing in Christ, they encountered little opposition – though Archbishop Egilbert of Mainz did try to save the city's Jews – in a world that was groping for fresh structures. They turned out to be particularly dangerous in that they supplied a catastrophic example, which was to be followed by similarly murderous explosions in the thirteenth and fourteenth centuries. New marginal, criminal elements would emerge to man the anti-Jewish demonstrations that accompanied the development of towns in response to the tensions arising out of that development. The instigators on this occasion, however, were the social and political authorities of those towns and even the ecclesiastical hierarchy, spreading a terrifying motivation based on aiming at the exclusion of the Jews.

The answer to the thorny question of whether anti-Semitism has Christian roots needs to be spread out over history. For many centuries the Jew was the Christian's memory; his presence was seen as being morally necessary to the Christian world, which confessed the 'true faith'. The Jew was therefore tolerable. Indeed, indulgence of the few might even be taken as far as respect for his originality in society. But the same period that saw the first wave of mass persecution break out against the Jews also saw the emergence of an anti-Jewish polemic that combined the teaching of contempt for Jews with systematic degradation of them. Old themes – the degeneration of Judaism since the birth of Christ, the infidel people incapable of understanding Scripture, the people that had killed God – were taken up again and expanded on.

On the Jewish side bitterness reigned, mingled after Salomon bar Simson had written his account of the First Crusade with cries for a vengeance that it was left to God to provide and with commemorative eulogies of the martyrs. Rabbinic writings placed the emphasis on the divine recompense to come and on the dignity of the Jewish people in this vale of tears. The Jewish communities, however much in a minority they were, scattered throughout the West, enjoyed a high level of culture. This was available to all members as a result of their being taught to read and write the holy language, and it was underpinned by a body of ordered, unchanging ritual. It gave them a deep sense of their own spiritual importance. At the same time Jewish piety acquired fresh vigour as first the Sephardic and then the Cabbalistic movements in Aragon and the Languedoc and Pietism in Germany and Champagne encouraged Jewish communities to lay claim to their spiritual dignity and particularity in terms of direct access to the truth.

From the late eleventh century onwards the economic conversion of the Jews proceeded apace and was soon complete. Excluded from the feudal system in rural areas, they flocked to the towns; likewise excluded from the administration of the emergent municipalities, they devoted themselves to commerce. Here was a fresh source of conflict in the new urban society that was beginning to assert itself. The only security for Jewish communities lay in direct subservience to the royal or imperial power at the cost of increasingly exorbitant fiscal and other demands. These *servi camerae*, more or less protected by the power of the monarch, came to be housed in separate districts, where they were obliged to reside. They wore distinguishing marks and were excluded from a long list of trades. They turned mainly to usury and became useful partners in the expanding monetary economy, albeit held in contempt and execrated because Christians were forbidden to lend money at interest. The Jews were thus tightly restricted and shifted to the margin of society.

From the thirteenth and fourteenth centuries onwards the

mental attitudes of urban and rural populations alike were characterized both publicly and privately by a sense of insecurity that called for defences, and one such defence was a pronounced anti-Semitism. A whole mythology of hatred developed, with accusations of desecration of the Host, ritual murder, well-poisoning and so on. It took only a slight provocation to unleash a mob against the Jews, their dwellings and their wealth. In the autumn of 1285, when one Christian child died in Munich, a presumed ritual murder victim, a total of 133 Jews were burnt. When the Black Death swept through Europe in 1349, in the towns and cities of Germany it was attributed to Jews having poisoned people's food and drink. Persecution broke out, Jews were increasingly expelled from certain areas and denied entry to others, and the ghettos of the West emptied, particularly those in England and France but subsequently those in the Germanic countries as well.

The Ashkenazic Jews began a different kind of marginal existence, this time on the margins of Western Europe, where Austria, Bohemia, Hungary and Poland all welcomed Jewish immigrants from the beginning of the thirteenth century onwards. The influx was considerable and continued into the fourteenth century. A fresh wave of persecutions in the Germanic countries in the fifteenth century increasingly pushed Jews in the direction of the kingdom of Poland. Rabbi Meisterlin of Wiener Neustadt wrote that 'the state of Cracovia and neighbouring areas have long formed a refuge for the expelled.' A series of royal privileges, initiated in 1263 and codified in the fourteenth century, created a legal framework there for the next three centuries. The mutual perception of the country welcoming Jews to this part of Europe and that of the Jews who settled there did not assume developed forms until modern times. Suffice it to say that in the fifteenth century the image of the infidel Jew as forged in the West and propagated by churchmen through their writings existed in the host countries too. However, the actual situation there was very much more favourable. In certain respects it was reminiscent of that of the early Medieval period in the West.

In the territories of the kingdom of Poland and the grand duchy of Lithuania, which came under the same monarch, Jews were exempt from the bondage, the *servitus Iudaeorum*, that was their lot in the West. They were treated as free subjects of the king, and for this reason Rabbi Solomon Luria, writing in the sixteenth century, regarded them as akin to nobles (*parashim*). Occasionally Jews would take up arms to defend a town alongside the Christians, showing the spontaneous solidarity of people facing a common danger. They took the oath *more Iudaico*, close to the synagogue, without any form of words that was offensive to them, such as was usual in the West.

In everyday life, social practices remained varied and contradictory. The fourteenth and fifteenth centuries saw instances of anti-Jewish rioting, sometimes fanned by zealous visiting preachers from the West – men like Giovanni di Capistrano. Such excesses were seen only in the large towns of the period – Kraków and Poznań, for example. Competition in handicrafts and in commerce gave rise to bans of a more provisional than permanent nature in certain fields of activity. Expulsions were few, the only effective ones being two from Warsaw in the fifteenth century. There were no closed ghettos, no exclusively 'Jewish' streets. A mixed quarter – Kazimierz, near Kraków – became an important economic centre. Everywhere there were notable successes in commerce and credit in which the complementarity of the Jewish presence in the urban network was increasingly evident. These successes gave the Polish and Lithuanian Jews a fairly solid base and a position that was the envy of their co-religionists in other countries.

Neighbourly relations between Jews and Christians – of various rites in these countries – in no way abolished the religious and cultural division between them but, local vicissitudes notwithstanding, did create a certain tacit cooperation on both sides. Jews in Poland and Lithuania read Hebrew and spoke Yiddish amongst themselves, though they also used Polish and Old Russian. The church continued to call for segregation and cultivated the Christicide image. In the fifteenth century it propagated the cult of Corpus Christi, and many new churches were given a dedication that carried strong anti-Jewish connotations drawn from the mythology obsession with desecration of the Host. Bishops and members of the lower clergy were reluctant to have constant recourse to the financial services provided by the Jews. There were conversions, sometimes forced by circumstances, sometimes voluntary, but the converts continued to associate with their compatriots. Jan-Abraham Ezofowicz converted around 1488, was ennobled, and became Treasurer of the grand duchy of Lithuania, yet he ran things with the help of two brothers of his who had remained loyal to Judaism. In fact the best aid to understanding the condition of the Jews in Eastern Central Europe in late Medieval and early modern times is the largely pluralistic composition of the states dominated by the Jagellonian dynasty. Populated by Poles, Germans, southern and north-eastern Ruthenians (ancestors of the Ukrainians and Byelorussians), Lithuanians, and in lesser numbers by Jews, Karaites, Tartars, Armenians, Wallachians and Italians, these territories accepted a *de facto* toleration based on respect for a variety of faiths, forms of worship, cultures and customs. These different majorities and minorities – including the Jews – lived and worked together.

As far as the Jews were concerned, there was always a feeling of self-affirmation, based on the special nature of the chosen people. The Talmudic standards required barriers to be observed between Jews and non-Jews. A lofty ideal was propagated by rabbinic responses to the problems of ritual and everyday life, and the same ideal can be traced from sepulchral inscriptions. A spirit of cohesion was maintained that surrounded the sometimes very small Jewish communities scattered throughout the country. Actual conditions continued to be favourable in comparison with those obtaining in other countries north of the Alps. Nevertheless, they could not cut the knot so tragically tied centuries before – a knot made up on the one hand of the hostility and envy surrounding a minority whose destiny it was to be of often major usefulness to members of the surrounding society and on the other of the incompatibility of what had become virtually impenetrable spiritual cultures. Not entirely, though: a Jew named Zul was a member of the Societas Vistulana, a circle of humanist intellectuals in Kraków in 1488–9; and there is some trace of penitential, mystical influences stemming from a different kind of spirituality in the rabbinic teachings of the disciples of Iehuda Hachasaid.

However, the interchange of action and reaction between the Christian majority and the Jewish minority was characterized by an inflexibility that allowed few concessions. Even in relatively tolerant countries, this legacy of the early Middle Ages still weighs heavily today.

Translated from the French by J. A. Underwood

SELECT BIBLIOGRAPHY

S. W. Baron, *A social and religious history of the Jews*, 16 vols, Princeton, 1957.

B. Blumenkranz, *Juifs et chrétiens dans le monde occidental 430–1096, Etudes Juives* 2, Paris – La Haye, 1960.

J. Katz, *Exclusiveness and Tolerance: Studies in Jewish History*, Oxford, 1961.

Germania Judaica I, Tübingen, 1963.

L. Finkelstein, *Jewish Selfgovernment in the Middle Ages*, New York, 1964.

G. Kisch, *Zur Rechtsstellung der Juden im Mittelalter, Zeitschrift der Savigny–Stiftung*, 1964, pp. 358–65.

L. Dasberg, *Untersuchungen über die Entwertung des Juden-Status im 11. Jh.*, La Haye, 1965.

Etudes sur le Judaisme médiéval, D. R. Blumenthal (ed.), 12 vols, Leiden, 1969–85.

Bernard D. Weinryb, *The Jews of Poland. A Social and Economic History of The Jewish Community in Poland from 1100–1800*, Philadelphia, 1973.

M. Kriegel, *Les Juifs à la fin du Moyen Age*, Paris, 1978.

Gli Ebrei nell'alto medioevo, Settimane di studio 26, 1980, Spoleto 1980, (contributions by L. Cracco Ruggini, J. Orlandis, G. I. Langmuir, A. Gieysztor, A. Grabois, B. Blumenkranz.

Christen und Juden in Offenbarung und kirchlichen Erklärungen vom Urchristentum bis zur Gegenwart, E. Weinzierl (ed.), Wien, 1988 (contribution by F. Graus).

Mutual Perceptions of Jews and Christians in Recent History

JACOB KATZ

The mutual perceptions of Jews and Christians in recent history may be analyzed by comparison with the analogous situation in previous epochs: in particular in the Middle Ages, and for as long as thought and feeling continued to be formed by religious traditions.[1]

It is true that in those times there were occasions when the members of both religions met each other on a purely human level – or rather, as incumbents of certain social roles. Even so, when a Christian who found himself short of funds asked a Jew for a loan, or when he let a Jewish doctor tend to him in his sickness, he never forgot the religious chasm that divided them.

Yet the encounter in such cases was governed by the practical necessities of the moment, and religious opposition retreated into the background. There, admittedly, the image formed by the traditional conception of the nature of the other was always present. In Jewish eyes, the Christian was a representative of the ruling society, which just about tolerated the Jew in its midst as a member of a deviant religion. In Christian eyes the Jew was foreign, not only in his religion, but also in his cultural pattern, his language and his entire view of the world. If the Christian participated to some extent in his own religious tradition, then he knew that the Jew belonged to a nation, from which the founder of his religion, the Son of God, had come. The founder had addressed his mission to his fellow-Jews, who, however, had refused to follow him, and were indeed responsible for his death. This explained the special position of the Jews at the periphery of Christian society.

The members of each community must have had a minimal sense of the relationship between them. At a high level, entire theological and legal systems were developed on each side, mutually exclusive of the other. On the Jewish side, absolute monotheism was stressed; on the Christian side the doctrine of the Trinity. Against the Christian belief in the historical fact of redemption through Christ, the Jews juxtaposed their expectations of the coming of a redeeming Messiah. Each religious community obliged its members to limit their occasional contacts with those of the other community. In all cases, the social symbiosis between Jews and Christians cannot simply be understood as the relationship between an indigenous majority and an immigrant minority. Both parties believed in an historical link which bound them together and at the same time determined their mutual rejection. The relationship was thus full of ambivalences, which could, however, be overcome thanks to the medieval belief that existential contradictions could be reconciled by dialectical reflection.

At the threshold of modernity, at the turn of the eighteenth century, the theoretical basis of the traditional position of the Jews within Christian society collapsed. The theological assumptions, which made possible the coexistence of relative toleration with mutual negation, were undermined by rationalistic and historical criticism. This critical approach was developed by individual thinkers and taken up by an intellectual élite in a more or less radical form. Depending on how radical the critical approach was, differing conclusions were drawn about what the attitude to the Jews should be. The radicals expected a complete rejection of religious traditions, Jewish as well as Christian, which would lead to the elimination of both religious communities from society. Once this situation was achieved, it followed that the constrictions imposed by each community on its members, based as they were on conflicting religious beliefs, would inevitably disappear. This expectation could already be found in the works of Voltaire; it was developed to its logical conclusion in the following generations by Bruno Bauer, Karl Marx and others.[2]

Adherents of this theory were also to be found within the Jewish community. At the beginning of the 1840s, the founders of the Society of Friends of Reform in Frankfurt advocated, it is true, only a removal of restrictions for the further development of the Jewish religion. Yet their silent hope was that this development, which was thought of as parallel to a similar process among Christians, would lead to a fully secularized society, in which the differences between Jews and Christians would dissolve.[3]

The course of history has shown these expectations to be ultra-rationalist utopias. Even the hope of a neutralization of the influence of religion on the ordinary human relations of Jews and Christians proved to be unrealistic. Instead the real spirit of the age fostered not the eradication of religion from the life of societies but rather its displacement from other spheres of human existence, such as the economy, art, the state and even society itself.

According to the usual idea of the proper pattern of modern society, religion should have its own proper place in human life. Religion, according to this view, serves to satisfy the human need for an ultimate metaphysical meaning of earthly existence. That does not, however, justify the exercise by religion, as it did in the Middle Ages, of the function of law-giver and adviser in all other areas of human activity. Those extra-religious spheres, such as the economy, the state, the arts and so on, should develop and function according to their own laws. This trend, which is often characterized as secularization, also offered the prospect of a decisive effect on Christian–Jewish relations. If the extra-religious spheres of human activity were released from their subordination to religion, then there was no reason why Jews should participate in them any less than Christians.

This was the conclusion which, at least in principle, was arrived at. To it, the Jews certainly owed their equality under the law in the state, the achievement of which came to be known as emancipation.[4] The fundamental release of economic activity, the arts and the public expression of opinion from the control of religious authorities also enlarged Jewish participation in these spheres. This did not mean, however, that Jews and Christians were made completely equal in their choice of occupations, cultural patterns and associations, in line with the loudly proclaimed postulate of secularization. The precondition of such an outcome was the complete elimination of the continuing influence of religion on the other spheres of life. Each party, however, expected this elimination of the other.

The Jews insisted on the realization of the principle of equality, which meant disregarding religious origins in appointments to state posts, in access to economic opportunities, or in the admission to social circles and events. Christians, on the other hand, insisted on consistency on the part of the Jews. They ought first to abandon all those Jewish features which were traditionally associated with their religion. Only if the Jew had adapted his bearing and outlook to the Christian standard could he hope to be accepted in non-Jewish society. He would be entitled to equal consideration in the competition for political and economic positions only when the famous, or notorious, solidarity of the Jews as a group – which itself was a result of their religious principles – was given up. Both parties, then, were in opposition over the role which religion, Christian and Jewish, should play in the already secular society.

A further point has to be considered. Secularization was initiated in an intellectual élite, and as it spread to larger sectors of society it displaced religion from its previously dominant position. Religion, however, indeed in its traditional form, survived, at least in the outlook of a minority. In secular society this minority was the bearer of modern orthodoxy, among Christians as well as among Jews. This orthodoxy appeared modern because it used a contemporary vocabulary in the expression of its beliefs. At heart, however, it was still completely bound to the teachings and ideas of the respective traditions. As we have seen in both Christianity and Judaism, these teachings contained precepts about relations with adherents of the rival religion, and these mirrored the mutual rejection, or even condemnation, which had developed at a time of active rivalry between the two religions. It is no wonder, therefore, that these precepts troubled modern interpreters who aimed at mutual toleration. With all their loyalty to their traditions, however, neither Jews nor Christians could turn their backs on the widely recognized principle of religious toleration. How was this religious toleration to be reconciled with traditional teachings and precepts? Representatives of the Jewish and Christian religions had to face this question.

The spokesmen for the two religions were, of course, in different situations here. The Jewish interpreters had to adapt unconditionally to the process that had led to the acceptance of the Jews in the state. This led them to postulate the general equality of human beings. The fact that this idea was contrary to certain elements of the Jewish tradition could be accommodated only by reinterpretation and apologetics. The Jewish ethic which originated in Biblical and Talmudic times, as well as the legal precepts and moral obligations which were self-evidently based on these, were concerned initially only with the Jewish people. The relation to those outside the Jewish community had to be specially determined, and that in itself excluded equal treatment for aliens and settled inhabitants.

The usual example used to illustrate this state of affairs is the Old Testament prohibition against usury, which was only valid in reference to other Jews, and not with regard to non-Jews. In Talmudic times many such special laws were introduced against idolators, undoubtedly in order to keep the communities of believers from having social contact with them. Most of these laws had already been altered during the Middle Ages, when Jews had become a minority in the countries in which they lived and the surrounding population no longer consisted of heathens but of Christians and Muslims. This adaptation of the laws to the needs of the times was achieved by use of Talmudic dialectics, which permitted an alteration of the legal rules without touching the canonical text. A simple revision of the laws was, however, no longer sufficient in the new situation in which Jews were emancipated and became citizens of the state. A universal ethic was now demanded which recognized no difference in the obligations toward persons of different religious beliefs and origins.

Once this demand acquired self-evident validity, Jewish interpreters of the Talmudic law thought they had rediscovered it in their own religious texts.[5] This is not the place to describe the method which permitted this harmonization. Suffice it to say that scholars and thinkers of the first rank, such as Moritz Lazarus, the founder of folk-psychology, and Hermann Cohen, the neo-Kantian, were able to bring about such a harmonization with a good conscience, without deliberately falsifying their tradition.[6] Admittedly, these were men of independent minds, who did not feel unconditionally bound to the literal validity of the law. Yet the same could even happen to someone such as David Hoffmann, who taught at the orthodox rabbinical seminary in Berlin, and who was known as a traditional Biblical scholar and trained Talmudist. Hoffmann added a bit of historical erudition to his Talmudic dialectic, and in this way came to the same conclusion as his more liberal contemporaries.[7]

Another fundamental feature of Jewish tradition, the belief in Messianic redemption, which would put an end to exile, also came into conflict with the struggle for full citizenship in the state and integration into non-Jewish society. For liberal thinkers it was easy to transform the prophecy of national redemption into the realization of a utopia of universal human perfection. To their orthodox colleagues such an offhand treatment of the actual substance of tradition was anathema. Yet they too could not avert their minds from the fact that the expected, or already achieved, emancipation was undermining the sense of exile and banishment. Nor could they ignore the way in which the proverbial yearning of Jews for their land of origin was being used as an effective weapon by the opponents of emancipation. The need to reinterpret the Messianic doctrine thus became unavoidable, for internal and external reasons. Such a reinterpretation was indeed carried out; this led to a dilution of the doctrine's meaning, so that it became merely the yearning for a spiritual elevation which would take place in the land of the fathers, at a time chosen by God.[8]

The acceptance of the Jews as citizens also caused problems for Christian theologians. After all, the exile of the Jews, evident in the exclusion of the exiles from political rights, was interpreted as a sign of their repudiation by God. The domination which had been transferred to the peoples of Christendom was thus seen as a proof of the truth of their religion. The elevation of Jews to citizenship would contradict this view.

There were indeed opponents of the emancipation of the Jews; they based their arguments on the Christian church's teaching about the subjugation of the Jews. Shortly before the French Revolution the academy of Metz organized a competition on the question of whether the Jews in France could be made into happier and more useful people. According to one theologian, the political and social elevation of the Jews was in fact possible, but in that case the Christian church, which based itself on the degradation of the Jews, would have to renounce one of the testaments to its truth.[9]

Even after equal political rights had been granted to Jews, Christian theologians still expressed their reservations. This is what the leading representatives of Catholic France, such as Gabriel de Bonald, Félicité de Lamennais and others, did during the Restoration.[10] The reluctance of the church to accept the political equality of the Jews was often justified by Jewish converts, of whom there were an especially large number in France, and who, as convinced Christians, placed themselves at the service of the church. One of their number,

Joseph Lemann, who knew a great deal about Jewish–Christian relations, provided an historical foundation for his views; he saw the emancipation of the Jews as an event made possible by the Revolution. In the *ancien régime*, according to Lemann, the Jews could rise to some extent in society, but they could never be incorporated into the body politic of the state, interwoven as it was with religion.[11] Since Catholic thinkers damned the Revolution as a deviation from the Christian path, the emancipation of the Jews could simply be counted among the sins of the revolutionaries.

The religious dogmatism of converts from Judaism in arguing against Jewish emancipation was not limited to Catholic France. A Protestant convert, Dr Wolfgang B. Fränkel, from southern Germany, pleaded with his brothers in 1842 to stop harbouring the illusion that they could merit acceptance by the state and society merely by adapting their religion to the spirit of the times. Even after all the changes of modern times, the foundations of public life were Christian, and only the members of the Christian churches were entitled to participate.[12]

This view was represented at a much higher level by the most important convert of the age, Friedrich Julius Stahl.[13] Stahl's argument also shows that Christian tradition could likewise be adapted to the dominant intellectual outlook. Stahl's views of emancipation were expressed in 1847 when the Jews in Prussia already possessed a considerable share of civil rights, such as the free choice of residence and occupation. The question of the day was whether Jews could participate in the leadership and administration of the state, in other words whether they should be allowed to have the active and passive franchise, and be appointed as civil servants. Stahl, who was at that time professor at the University of Berlin and an exponent of conservative ideas in political theory and jurisprudence, argued in a most convoluted way for securing the position the Jews had already reached, and at the same time for withholding the political rights which they still sought. The state which defined itself as Christian could allow those of other faiths, indeed even those without faith, to live freely within its bounds, but their participation in politics and administration would contradict its nature. This had, therefore, to be prevented. The readiness of this sharp-witted thinker to compromise is perhaps to be explained by his sympathetic concern for the fate of the members of his own race, whom he knew well.

The Prussian conservatives, whose ideological representative Stahl had become, maintained their reservations about all aspects of Jewish emancipation, even after its official provision in the constitution of the newly formed German Empire. Fundamental and enduring reservations about the Jewish claims for equality were those of a minority. The predominant view, at least until the emergence of the anti-Semitic movement at the end of the 1870s, was that the social division between Jews and Christians should disappear with progressive secularization. In reality, however, the members of both religious communities continued in great measure to live and work separately from each other, and remained in the circles where they had been born.

The question of religious differences did not cease to be of public interest; the intellectual exponents of both religions continued to discuss them. The only difference was that now, unlike in the Middle Ages, they no longer debated the truth of dogmas and the correct interpretation of Holy Scriptures. Rational and historical criticism had pushed these questions into the background, even for the faithful. What was fought over was, as it were, the 'by-products' of the religions, their moral teachings, their philosophical assumptions – in other words, the traces which they would leave behind, even after the rejection of their dogmatic substance.[14]

There was also a shift in the balance of forces of the several communities compared to earlier times. In the past, Jewish participants in the debate were usually inhibited from speaking freely against the established religion. Even Moses Mendelssohn had consciously set himself limits in his famous dispute with the proselytizing Johann Caspar Lavater.[15] In the nineteenth century, however, the religious spokesmen of Judaism thought themselves free to expound their views openly. This was a right of which they made much use, not always within the limits prescribed, but always to the vexation and exasperation of their opponents. The belief in the superiority of Christianity in all aspects was so deeply rooted in the collective consciousness that any Jewish objection to that superiority was regarded as presumptuous. This was so even for Christians whose attachment to their religion was anything but dogmatic.

Even when the debate was conducted on both sides by persons who were free of dogmatism, as was by then mostly the case, they usually based their arguments on traditional teachings and on the canonical texts. Was the New Testament, from the standpoint of universal human values such as a rational understanding of the world and a positive affirmation of life, a step forward or a step back? Were the moral teachings proclaimed by Jesus in the Sermon on the Mount an original contribution or rather an amalgam of Pharisaic precursors, with a dash of ascetic exaggeration and utopian ethical rigorism?[16]

The answers to the questions thus formulated were constricted for both parties by their first principles. There was by no means an open dialogue, in which the participants were prepared to learn from each other. Despite the rationalistic approach, the standards by which one judged one's own religion and that of one's interlocutor were quite different, as Gustav Landauer occasionally remarked. The value of one's own religion was measured on the basis of its original ideal or its idealized intention; the religion of the other party was judged in accordance with the outward form it had acquired in the course of its historical development.[17] Instead of mutual understanding and reconciliation these debates produced mutual irritation, and the Jewish side was plainly fated to come off the poorer. Despite the formal freedom of expression of beliefs, the public criticism of Christianity by Jews was not looked on at all kindly. In contrast, the right to devalue

Judaism remained unchallenged. We can recognize in this situation what was doubtless a half-conscious remnant of the status of the Jews as a pariah-community.

The spokesmen for the Jewish cause in the nineteenth century were apt to describe their situation by saying that the Jews had been emancipated, but not Judaism. They meant by this that the Jewish religion was not given the same recognition and support by the state as the Christian religion was. Thus, for instance, setting up a chair in Jewish theology at one of the universities was stubbornly prohibited.[18] This observation has a less obvious but no less important meaning. Not only in official decisions, but also in the spontaneous expressions of public opinion, the Jewish religion was always liable to be disparaged. This can clearly be seen in the behaviour of the Christian participants in controversies with Jews. Only seldom did they bother to answer the substance of Jewish objections. For the most part, the Jewish questioners were rebuked as hardly being worthy of an answer. This is reminiscent of the attitudes of the Viennese student corporations, who declared their Jewish classmates to be unqualified to 'give satisfaction' in duels, and for that reason decided that Jews' challenges to duels should be refused.

The question arises as to whether there was a way to ease the tension which was more or less latent in relations between secularized Jews and Christians. Many persons of good will believed there was a chance to unite the two camps. Christians who regarded their attachment to Christianity more as a cultural inheritance than as a religious tie, cherished this hope. The increasing cultural adaptation of the Jews to their non-Jewish environment encouraged the view that this would lead to their adherence to Christianity.

At the individual level, this possibility seemed to be supported by the conversion of many Jews to Christianity. These Jewish converts did indeed regard this step as the completion of their acculturation, or at least they justified it as such. Admittedly this occurred mainly among intellectuals, especially academics, who must have seen baptism as a precondition for professional advancement. Yet it was precisely the concomitants of such occurrences which showed that this sort of solution was not generally practicable. For such decisions were often made with a bad conscience, since an ultimately secular goal was being attained through a religious action. As a result many who faced such an alternative recoiled from following it, even though they had no dogmatic attachment to Judaism.

It was easy for Franz Brentano to recommend baptism to the young Hugo Bergmann as the way to an academic career, on the grounds that the lack of a baptismal certificate was nothing more than a 'purely external obstacle'.[19] The advice of Leopold von Ranke to the gifted pupil Harry Breslau has a similar ring to it: 'What is stopping you converting? You are already historically a Christian.'[20] Theodor Mommsen recommended that Jews not bound by any religious belief should become converts to Christianity as an actual condition for their incorporation into the German nation.[21]

Most of those who gave such advice were secularized Christians who could not imagine that remnants of the Jewish religion had survived in the minds of secular Jews, as remnants of Christianity had survived in their own minds. Since this was the case, however, the expectation of assimilation into Christianity as the ultimate result of cultural adaptation proved illusory.

The expectations of Jewish intellectuals, who had hoped for a unification with Christendom on the basis of, so to speak, a revision of religious history, proved mistaken for similar reasons. Historical research had shown, or at least claimed to show, the extensive dependence of the teachings of Jesus on Jewish sources. One could deduce intellectually that Jesus would be claimed as a part of the Jewish cultural achievement. If the founder of the Christian religion was thus placed in the succession of Jewish thinkers or even of the prophets, then the historical conflict between Judaism and Christianity must have been a tragic misunderstanding. This insight should have resulted in a common reverence for Jesus on the part of both Jews and Christians. This at least was the argument of Constantin Brunner, which he tirelessly advanced with the passion of one possessed.[22]

This expectation ignored the difference between intellectual assessment and religious and cultural reverence. Of the person and teaching of Jesus only the former is accessible to the Jew. The latter can only be achieved truly through a genuine conversion. To the Jew who has not become a convert, the encounter with Christian worship is an embarrassment which he will very wisely avoid, and which an understanding Christian will not expect of him.

I shall end by illustrating this point with a personal experience of mine. In Jerusalem I am a member of the Rainbow Group, an association at which Jews and Christians meet monthly to discuss contemporary or historical matters related to religion. The evening programme consists of a lecture with a discussion to follow. In order, however, to lend the event a certain sanctity, a text of some spiritual, if not precisely religious, content is read at the beginning and another at the end of the evening, one chosen and read by a Jew, the other by a Christian. The lectures often have to do with the religious differences between Jews and Christians and these are the subject of free discussion. No one at all would think of avoiding Jewish or Christian teachings and symbols in the lectures, but during the readings, which provide a sort of frame for the evening and give everyone there a feeling of belonging together, there is always some reticence. As far as I can remember, no Christian has ever selected a text in which the name of Jesus or any other such obviously Christian symbol or concept occurred. It is not as though this has been laid down in the statutes of the association, nor as though the issue has ever been discussed. Rather, Christian members have a spontaneous, tactful appreciation of the need to spare the Jewish participants any embarrassment. The Christians often choose texts from Jewish scriptures, not only from the Hebrew Bible, but also from Talmudic sources, and from the post-exilic period. The mutual relationship of Jews and Christians is, therefore, asymmetrical. The Christians can allow the contents of Jewish tradition to influence them, to the extent that they are relevant. For Jews, on the other hand, the central symbols of Christianity have, as a result of the meanings they have acquired in the course of their history, lost their religious, existential and philosophical accessibility, even though they retain their intellectual meaning. The realization that this is so is a precondition for a relaxed and fruitful encounter between believing, and even half-secular, Jews and Christians.

Translated from the German by Steven Beller

NOTES

[1] See Jacob Katz, *Exclusiveness and Tolerance: Studies in Jewish–Gentile Relations in Medieval and Modern Times*, Oxford, 1961.

[2] Jacob Katz, *Vom Vorurteil bis zur Vernichtung. Der Antisemitismus 1700–1933*, Munich, 1989, caps. 3 (Voltaire), 13 (*Die Radikalen*. Feuerbach, Bauer, Marx).

[3] Michael Meyer, 'Alienated intellectuals in the camp of religious reform, the Frankfurt Reformfreunde 1842–5', in *AJS Review* VI (1981), pp. 61–85.

[4] Jacob Katz, *Aus dem Ghetto in die bürgerliche Gesellschaft. Jüdische Emanzipation 1770–1870*, Frankfurt, 1986.

[5] See Katz, *Exclusiveness and Tolerance*, caps. 13–14.

[6] Moritz Lazarus, *Die Ethik des Judentums*, 2 vols. Frankfurt a.M. 1898, 1911; Hermann Cohen, 'Das Problem der jüdischen Sittenlehre. Eine Kritik von Lazarus' Ethik des Judentums', in *Jüdische Schriften* 3, Berlin, 1924, pp. 1–35.

[7] David Hoffmann, *Der Schulchan Aruch und die Rabbiner über das Verhältnis der Juden zu den Andersgläubigen*, Berlin, 1885.

[8] This view can be seen already in Moses Mendelssohn, see Jacob Katz, *Zur Assimilation und Emanzipation der Juden*, Darmstadt, 1982, p. 70.

[9] Katz, *Aus dem Ghetto* (note 4), pp. 85–6.

[10] Discussed in detail in Katz, *Vom Vorurteil* (note 2), pp. 197–200.

[11] Joseph Lemann, *L'entrée des Israélites dans la société française et les états chrétiens*, Paris, 1886, pp. 298–336.

[12] Wolfgang B.Fränkel, *Die Unmöglichkeit der Emanzipation der Juden im christlichen Staate*, Elberfeld, 1842.

[13] See Katz, *Vom Vorurteil* (note 2), pp. 197–200.
[14] See Jacob Katz, 'Judaism and Christianity against the background of modern secularism', in *Jewish emancipation and self-emancipations*, Philadelphia, 1986, pp. 34–48. The confrontation between the two religions in modern times is discussed in detail in Uriel Tal, *Christians and Jews in Germany in the Second Reich*, Ithaca, 1975.
[15] Alexander Altmann, *Moses Mendelssohn, a biographical study*, Alabama, 1973, pp. 209–23.
[16] See note 14.
[17] See Franz Rosenzweig, *Zweistromland*, Berlin, 1926, p. 73.
[18] Monika Richarz, *Der Eintritt der Juden in die akademischen Berufe*, Tübingen, 1984, pp. 192–3.
[19] Schmuel Hugo Bergmann, *Tagebücher und Briefe 1901–1948* I, Königstein, 1985, p. 42. Bergmann's answer is in ibid. pp. 43–4.
[20] Related by Friedrich Meinecke. See Pinchas E. Rosenblüth, 'Friedrich Meineckes Anschauung über Juden und Judentum', in *Bulletin des Leo Baeck Instituts*, 1975, p. 109.
[21] Theodor Mommsen, *Auch ein Wort über unser Judentum*, Berlin, 1880. Printed in W. Böhlich, *Der Berliner Antisemitenstreit*, Frankfurt, 1965, pp. 176–9.
[22] See my article, note 14.

The Jew as Enemy and as Neighbour: The Paradox of Christian Anti-Semitism

JAN BŁOŃSKI

In the spring of 1942 the Polish resistance became aware of Hitler's real objective, namely the extermination of the Jews. In order to bring the full horror of the situation home to the populace, that August a group of leading figures of the Polish underground published a pamphlet. Written by Zofia Kossak, a well-known and respected Roman Catholic novelist, it was hawked around in large numbers. I should like to quote a few sentences from it.

After explaining the situation, Zofia Kossak draws the following conclusions:

That is why we Polish Catholics are speaking out. Our feelings towards the Jews have not changed. We still regard them as political, economic and spiritual [*ideowi*] enemies of Poland. What is more, we are aware that they hate us more than they hate the Germans, that they hold us responsible for their misfortunes . . . However, the existence of these feelings in no way absolves us from our duty to condemn this crime . . . Anyone who remains silent in the face of murder becomes an accomplice of the murderer; anyone who does not condemn, gives his consent.

The writer then goes on to implore her compatriots and coreligionists to give assistance to the Jews without shrinking from the punishment they risk in so doing.

It is a curious text, possibly even difficult to understand nowadays. It is rarely referred to, and then somewhat shamefacedly and for disparate ends: either to point out that Jews were helped even by Poles who hated them, or alternatively to show that even the Poles who decided to help Jews did so with reluctance. My reason for recalling it is simply that I wish to try to reconstruct the moral and intellectual climate that made such a clash of ideas and values possible.

First, however, let me make two points. Witnesses assure us that Zofia Kossak did not in fact harbour such violently hostile feelings towards the Jews herself; she worded her appeal in the way she did in order to anticipate – as pithily and unambiguously as possible – the kinds of objection that might be raised and to underline the absolute, imperative nature of the duty to help the Jews. That is possible – even probable. But it makes little difference as far as we are concerned. Indeed, the contradiction simply leaves the confines of an individual mind to reappear in the collective consciousness. On the other hand I feel bound to state that Zofia Kossak did commit herself vigorously to helping her 'enemies' and that several dozen Jews – if not more – directly owed or owe their lives to her. Such courage and self-sacrifice make any kind of *ad personam* criticism improper.

What, then, of the text? It is written in the name of the 'Catholic Poles'. The expression *Polak katolik* was constantly on the lips of spokesmen of the right-wing National Democratic party, which made no secret of its anti-Semitism – quite the reverse. The pamphlet is clearly aimed at that kind of public. Of the two elements it is undoubtedly the Catholic who is obliged to come to the aid of the Jew; the Pole does so solely because he is by definition Catholic. In other words, the argument in favour is essentially a religious one. The Gospel message is contrasted with secular interests (which the author does not pass over in silence). It speaks clearly of 'loving your neighbour' – the hardest of all the Commandments. More than that, the blindness and injustice of the Jews ('they hate us more than they hate the Germans') seem, for Zofia Kossak, to constitute an additional reason for helping them. Indeed, the more wicked your enemy, the greater your merit in giving your life for him. And let us not forget for one moment that that is precisely what was at stake; in Poland, any kind of assistance rendered to Jews carried the death penalty.

Initially, then, what we see here is a contradiction that was felt painfully at the time by a great many people, including representatives of the anti-Semitic right. I refer to the difficulty – not to say impossibility – of reconciling nationalism with Christianity. If we look more closely, however, we find something rather deeper than this. The Jews are labelled enemies of Poland – political and economic enemies, but also spiritual or intellectual enemies. A spiritual enmity peculiar to Jews as a whole can only – it would seem – follow from the Jewish religion. So we find this line of argument picking up the thread of traditional Christian anti-Semitism. Potentially, at least, the injunction to help the Jews takes on an apologetic connotation in that it appears to prove the superiority of the New Testament over the Old. The author may not in fact have meant the epithet 'spiritual' in that way. What is certain is that holding their faults or sins against those one is in the act of helping – in other words, dispensing humiliation at the same time as one is offering assistance – is pharisaical behaviour of the first order.

A few words are thus all it takes to make a local nationalism conflict with Christian universalism, just as traditional Christian anti-Semitism conflicts with the Gospel message with which Zofia Kossak is so passionately concerned to keep faith. However, there is a third presence in the text, a presence that emphasizes the difference between traditional, Christian anti-Semitism and pagan, totalitarian anti-Semitism. This third person says nothing; he is content simply to kill – first the Jew, then whoever comes to the Jew's aid. He kills in response to a 'scientific' doctrine, thanks to which the world will soon be purged of evil (viz., the Jews).

It is the presence of this third person that casts such a dark shadow over the pamphlet. Regarding the Jews as enemies, it appears to accept that there is some truth in the Nazi propaganda – while nevertheless drawing diametrically opposite conclusions. One is entitled to wonder who could have followed Kossak's line of reasoning – surely only people capable of understanding the moral paradox whereby the wickedness of the Jews became an – additional – argument that it was thought would encourage people to help them. As for the majority, there was a good chance of Zofia Kossak's words providing an excuse for their indifference. Whatever the writer's intentions, then, what she wrote was potentially scandalous.

But of course the Jews were not 'enemies of Poland'. That is why we have to think again about why Zofia Kossak believed there could never be an understanding with the Jews. After writing that the Jews 'hold us responsible for their misfortunes', she cannot resist adding: 'Why, for what reason, remains a mystery of the Jewish mind.' One has the feeling that she sees any attempt at communication as doomed. It is not enough to blame this on 'nationalism'. The word has many meanings, and in any case the author has just shown that she does not regard the 'nation' as the supreme value. So should we perhaps be looking at the 'spiritual' enmity? It is not impossible.

First let us make one further attempt to follow Zofia Kossak's way of thinking. She observed that Jewish shopkeepers were in competition with Christian shopkeepers, that there were Jews who felt little attachment to the Polish state, and so on. In a nutshell, she saw increasing interpenetration of individual and collective interests within a shared social space. She also saw the increasingly violent conflicts to which that interpenetration gave rise. With her provincial aristocratic background, which was not particularly anti-Semitic – rather the reverse – and her preoccupation with the past (she wrote mainly historical novels), Zofia Kossak was probably incapable of understanding other solutions to such problems than those that had already been tried.

Feudal society had always tended to separate – by custom, by law and also by land distribution – social groups that might clash with one another. Why was Poland once regarded as a Jewish paradise? Because there Jews were able to live more apart than in other countries. Particularly east of the Vistula, where Jews were really numerous, the population was small, the social fabric relatively loose, the internal autonomy of the Jews total and their contacts with Christians limited and specialized. The *shtetl* might be a ghetto, but it was experienced as a place of liberty where people felt perfectly at home, the more so since living there was not actually compulsory. As an old nursery rhyme puts it:

> *Jedzie, jedzie pan na koniku sam,*
> *Sługa za nim ze śniadaniem,*
> *A za nimi Żyd, Żyd, Żyd, na koniku hyc, hyc, hyc!*
> *A za nimi chłop, chłop, chłop, na koniku hop, hop, hop!*

> (In front rides the lord, alone on his horse,
> Followed by his servant, bringing the breakfast,
> Then comes the peasant on his little horse,
> And then the Jew, hop, hop, hop – on horseback too!)

The Jew came last – but he had his horse, and he seemed happy enough.

So traditional anti-Semitism tended to separate. If necessary it resorted to banishment, as in West Europe. Totalitarian anti-Semitism exterminated, believing Jews in California to be as noxious as Jews in Berlin.

Zofia Kossak very probably thought about the problem on the basis of the idea of separation. The massive – and relatively recent – irruption of Jews into common society struck her as an invasion, whence the revolting stupidities of her pamphlet, stupidities that she may have felt were necessary to get her meaning across even to openly anti-Semitic readers. A very large proportion of the inhabitants of Central Europe – and not only Central Europe – thought as she did. Her wretched pamphlet expressed the – interestingly radical – moral consequences of that way of thinking. Zofia Kossak saw the Jews as enemies but was terrified by the persecution and, above all, by the threat of genocide. As far as she was concerned, the two reactions harmonized quite naturally; they posed no problem. She was incapable of seeing civil society in the same terms as we do. So she was prepared to give her life for the Jews. If, however, they had by some miracle been able to leave the country without suffering unduly, she would have felt nothing but relief, for she neither saw any need for, nor believed there to be any possibility of, genuine coexistence. One reason why we are here is to rise above and repudiate that way of seeing things.

Translated from the French by J. A. Underwood

The Challenge of Totalitarianism: Judaism and Christianity in Relation to Twentieth-Century Totalitarianism

JOZEF TISCHNER

This essay intends to present a framework for a dialogue between Judaism and Christianity on the subject of totalitarianism. Today both Jews and Christians are burdened by the memory of two totalitarianisms: Nazi totalitarianism and Communist totalitarianism, particularly its Stalinist variant. Although the experiences that were suffered arouse dread, they also force our consciences to be vigilant. They demand that every effort be made both to avoid a repetition of the tragedy and to extract some prospect of hope from the agonizing memories. Particular attention will be paid to the possibility of dialogue on a philosophical level since it is an undeniable task of intellectuals addressing the issue of totalitarianism to deprive it of its ideological legitimacy. A critique of totalitarian ideologies should be adequate to the nature of the particular ideologies in question. It is characteristic of these ideologies that they claim to be rational; and since totalitarianism cites science, rational philosophy and theory based on experience, philosophy is the only discipline which has the necessary means of countering these claims. Although criticism from a strictly religious or even theological standpoint cannot in principle be ruled out, it is in the nature of such criticism that it can only be conducted on a level that is accessible exclusively to the faithful; this automatically precludes any direct confrontation. This does not, however, mean that a philosophical critique of totalitarianism is incompatible with religion. The religious inspiration of philosophy must nonetheless be distinguished from the rational criteria which philosophy applies.

Although it would no doubt be interesting to consider possible ways in which the religious inspiration and rational thought in philosophy could be reconciled, this would constitute a wide digression from our subject. What we propose to do here is to set forth a critique of totalitarianism through the dialogue between Christian philosophy – particularly its Augustinian variant – and the so-called philosophy of dialogue which has – at least through two of its advocates Franz Rosenzweig and Emanuel Levinas – engaged in a radical critique of modern totalitarianism from the Jewish standpoint.

It is not just totalitarianism, however, that is the crucial issue at stake in the dialogue on totalitarianism. There comes a point at which we must raise the issue of the genuine meaning of our faiths – I say 'our' because they have evolved from a common origin – and of the attitude to the world of unbelief that has arisen from it. This attitude has polarized until now into two partly divergent standpoints: on the one hand were those, in the main Christians, who in their apostolic zeal attempted to bring about a 'synthesis' between the truths of the revelation and the wisdom of pagan knowledge, and on the other hand were those, in the main Jews, who out of concern for the treasures that had been delivered to them and them alone disassociated themselves from everything that was pagan, and lived on this earth as if they were lonely islanders. There was a certain danger inherent in both standpoints. Attempts at synthesis resulted in problematical compromise, and preoccupation with maintaining a distinctive identity led to isolation. The tragedy of totalitarianism and its unimaginable atrocities has convulsed both Jews and Christians and has led to the question whether compromise with the pagan world does not open the floodgates to totalitarianism, and whether preoccupation with personal spiritual excellence is not tantamount to the sin of passivity. In other words, we must ask whether we ourselves were not, through insufficient loyalty to our own heritage, directly or indirectly responsible for summoning up the evil spirits which spread throughout Europe. The possibility of such a conjecture raises the crucial issue of the significance of the faith of Abraham as a value both for us and for the world. In this way the dialogue on totalitarianism is gradually transformed into a dialogue on the essential nature of the common aspects of our faith.

I propose to discuss three issues. First, a clarification of the concept of totalitarianism is needed to provide a foundation for further analysis. Second, an evaluation of totalitarianism from the perspective of the basic tenets of the Judaeo-Christian tradition is also necessary. Only when we have done this will it be possible to enter upon a critique of totalitarianism. Finally, I will ask which experiences, concepts and beliefs common to both Judaism and Christianity can lay the basis for denying the claims of totalitarianism. It is only when these questions have been answered that it may be possible to illuminate the area of our common responsibility.

The Essence of Totalitarianism

Totalitarianism eludes simple definition since it is not clear whether it is to be viewed from the standpoint of those who exercise totalitarian power or from the standpoint of its subjects and especially its victims. It is an essential feature of totalitarianism that it does not allow any viewpoint other than its own; the consciousness of power and power itself permeate all things and tend to fill the framework in which power itself is to be thought about.

An analysis of the concept can serve as a starting-point. The word 'totalitarianism' is derived from the Latin 'totus' meaning 'whole' and it is worth examining the intentional meaning of this word when the suffix '-ism' is appended to it. The concept of totalitarianism denotes a system of exercising power in which that power, aiming to subjugate the whole person, claims to be the expression of a force which rules over the whole of reality and therefore has the right to use all and any means of coercion against its opponents. Totalitarianism is more than just tyranny or absolutism; the difference between them does not, however, lie in the extent of its lawlessness but in the way it seeks to legitimate its power. Power in a totalitarian regime presents itself as the expression of an absolute force which rules over everything in the territory in which it prevails, and which simultaneously claims that it and it alone possesses the knowledge necessary for the attainment of this objective. The omnipotence of power is the foundation of its claim to infallibility. Its belief in its infallibility reinforces its omnipotence.

There is a further aspect to the concept of totality. One of the consequences of totalitarian ideology is the thesis that all relations between one person and another can be reduced to the relationship of the part to the whole. This implies that all relations between human beings, including the most intimate, are subordinated to the interests of the 'whole' and in particular to the interests of the state. As a result, every close relationship becomes a relationship which must be controlled by the state; even friendship must have the approval of the state. The power of totalitarianism owes its success to the industrial age, and for this reason the concept of the whole and the part should be extended to include the image of a machine and its components, or even better the image of electricity and the billions of light bulbs and engines which it illuminates or sets in motion. It was Lenin, after all, who said that Communism equals Soviet power plus human beings and the relationships between them as instruments for its own end. Totalitarianism is a radical negation of the Kantian categorical imperative which asserts that the human being should always be an end in him or herself and not a means to the end of another person. The instrumentalization of the relationships of human beings would, nevertheless, appear to be more a consequence of totalitarianism than its principal tenet;

this derives from the entire ontology and epistemology which totalitarianism adduces to legitimate its claims.

Stalinism can serve as an example. Stalin defined the essence of historical materialism as follows: 'Historical materialism is the extension and application of the principles of dialectical materialism to the study of the phenomena of social life and of its history.'[1]

What does this 'extension' mean? It means that a dialectic describing the relations between objects is imposed on social dialogue. Dialectical materialism describes the dialectic of physical nature whereas historical materialism describes social life. Stalin therefore presupposed that the same processes which take place between physical objects such as atoms, also govern the relations among human beings. Dialogue, therefore, becomes dialectic. Objects are ranged in opposition to each other, and these opposing forces are in a state of collision with each other. A similar process occurs in the relations of human beings. Society is cloven by class conflict. All human beings belong to one or another class and cannot avoid involvement in the conflict. Hannah Arendt's thesis of the totalitarian instrumentalization of human relationships has to be modified. It is true that totalitarianism treats human beings as instruments. Stalinist totalitarianism tried to make human beings into a particular kind of instrument that would function as a weapon against other human beings; a human being is assimilated to an instrument with rather more resemblance to a tank or gun than a ploughshare or a hammer and sickle.

Totalitarianism therefore justifies itself first of all through an ontology. Its main argument can be expressed by the thesis: to have a real existence is to exercise power. Those who do not have power cannot be said to exist in any real sense. Martin Heidegger associated totalitarianism with the philosophy of Nietzsche's 'will to power'. In his study of Hegel, Franz Rosenzweig went even further back: he referred to Parmenides and his belief that all plurality is reduced to unity. Emanuel Levinas is no less radical in citing Heraclitus, for whom the true nature of being was manifested in war. But if it is to appeal to the masses, totalitarianism has to abandon ontological abstraction and to address them in a language which they understand. This is a language which stirs the sensitivity to the sacred and the human conscience. In this way totalitarian sacrology and ethics emerge alongside totalitarian ontology.

The sacred or the holy, according to the persuasive arguments of Rudolf Otto, is the supreme value. It endows all other values with meaning, and it transports the human being who encounters it into a state of fascination and dread. The sacred demands unreserved self-renunciation and sacrifice. The temptation of Abraham serves to illustrate the way in which the sacred works. God chose Abraham, and the fact that he was chosen placed Abraham in a dramatic conflict between God as the highest transcendental value and his son as the highest primordial value. The experience of the sacred demands that those who are dominated by the highest transcendental value have no right to the enjoyment of other values. This is parallel to the totalitarian claim, even though it originated in the experience of the sacred. Stalinism made the same demands, except that it was no longer God but the revolution which was the site of the sacred. The revolution demanded unlimited devotion and sacrifice. The new model of the revolutionary ideal was exemplified by the son who denounced his father since the father had been unmasked as an enemy of the revolution. It was no longer the father who led the son to the altar on the mountain where he was to be sacrificed but the son who led the father. The underlying drama in both situations is the same; the totalitarian principle has an identity with the relationships of the transcendental and the sacred.

The ethical legitimation of totalitarianism has a similar pattern. Anyone whose behaviour is governed by the conviction that his deeds serve to realize the highest ethical values acts with a good conscience. Totalitarian ideology aims to ensure that its agents, even if they are criminals, have a good conscience. It skilfully achieves this by manipulation which assigns high ethical values to political activity. Stalinism illustrated this very well: it assumed that the proper aim of political power was to eliminate the exploitation of man by man. This aim could be achieved only by violence. The new ethics therefore allowed the use of violence as the means to this end. Why should only evil be entitled to use force for the attainment of its ends? Why should the good be powerless? The new ethics engendered a new heroism. The revolutionary was not afraid to bear the onus of the use of violence because he believed that future generations would exonerate him from all guilt. Someone had to do the dirty work so that others could live in a better world. Such an ethic could be so persuasive that a person could have a good conscience for inflicting torture on others. There were even those who would take on themselves the guilt of others, bearing the punishment for deeds they had not committed so that the ennobled future would be more speedily attained. They justified their conduct by the argument that the truths of existence were disclosed to them in the performance of acts of violence. In doing so they participated in the sacred.

Ontological and ethical legitimation and the sacred reach their apogee in the concept of a total power which no human being and no sphere of life can evade. This vision is manifested most clearly in Stalinism which seeks to 'expropriate' and abolish private property as a condition for the 'socialization' of human beings. Since the power of one man over another is exerted through possession, the 'abolition' of private property is a prerequisite for the 'liberation' of man. In accordance with Marxist principles, Stalinism did not, however, aim to 'abolish' all property but only private property in the means of production. Private ownership of the means of production was not only intrinsically evil but it was also the source of all social evil. Through the 'socialization' of the means of production, totalitarian power was able to dominate the sphere of human labour and so ultimately became the owner of both labour and its product. It imposed limits on every manifestation of creativity in the sphere of work, and through its dominion over all labour, it also gained power over the entire human being. The attack on private property was only a means to an end: the object was the human being. In place of the 'old human being' the 'new human being' was to come forth. It was to be a 'human being' who had been divested of all acquisitive desires. This type of person was not to possess anything, not even himself. He had to be totally at the disposition of those who exercised power from which he was to draw the meaning of his existence.

No distinction can be drawn in totalitarianism between political power and the legitimation of that power: political power is not only power over the actions of individuals; it is also power over their thought and consciousness, and particularly over the way in which they think about power. The legitimation of power occurs at three levels – the ontological, the sacred and the ethical. Under totalitarianism, these three levels yield their autonomy to the demands of the totalitarian rulers. Science and human thought lose their autonomy and become instruments of totalitarian power in the war it wages against its real or imagined enemies. In totalitarianism truth does not exist as an objective value of human thought since 'truth' is whatever serves totalitarian power.

The Lure of Totalitarianism

The second issue is the assessment of totalitarianism from the basic Judaeo-Christian standpoint. The conclusion may be brief but the explanation that totalitarianism is the product of pagan religious belief requires more space. For the heirs of the faith of Abraham, in order to understand the significance of totalitarianism, the standpoint of paganism must be taken into account. The concept of paganism may, however, be too ambiguous to serve an explanatory purpose. Paganism is too complex a phenomenon for it to be considered here in any great detail: we are both the debtors and the heirs of this culture, while our attempts to understand it have been no less strenuous than our desire – albeit unsuccessful –

to escape from it. Only those aspects of paganism will be treated here which have been disclosed in a new light by the recent history of Communism.

Despite its unquestioned ambiguity, the concept of paganism served Europe for many centuries as a means of defining its own distinctive character. It had at first a negative connotation: anyone who was not a Jew or a Christian was a pagan. Pagans were excluded from the community of the chosen people and the community of the baptized, and were regarded as the enemies of both.

Since a negative interpretation is inadequate, a positive meaning must be sought. For reasons of geography and history the religion of ancient Greece and Rome served as the model of pagan religion for the Jews and Christians. On the question of how these religions conflicted with the faith of Abraham, an explanation can be found in the views of Rosenzweig and the interesting commentary on his views by Stefan Moses, which state that they differed by reason of their belief in *fatum* and their profound disbelief in the word, particularly the word denoting choice. Although the word could define the world, describe objects and express the tragic aspects of human life, it could not provide a basis for relationships among human beings, constitute loyalty or form a nation's history, and above all it had not the slightest relevance to religion. The word reached its highest point in the language of tragedy.

One of the consequences of a belief in *fatum* and a simultaneous disbelief in it is the acknowledgement that human fate is primarily governed by obscure subterranean forces which determine man's destiny without his having any influence on it. Whether it destroys or saves, *fatum* does so indifferently to the desires or efforts of those it affects. It follows that man's freedom is only an illusion of freedom. The human will is impotent. There is no lasting connection between 'willing' and 'acting'. It becomes impossible for one human being to make a permanent choice of another, or to remain loyal to the persons and values that he has chosen. The relationship between one person and another, for example between Oedipus and his father and mother, becomes like the relationships of material objects among themselves. Human beings – like physical objects – are connected with each other by chains of causality. Oedipus kills his father without knowing whom he is killing. He takes his mother as wife without knowing that she is his mother. The actions of Oedipus have a cause and an effect but it is not those that define the meaning of his deeds; that meaning is defined by *fatum* and it differs from that intended by Oedipus. It is fate which separates people or brings them together. Dialogue therefore becomes nothing more than a multi-voiced soliloquy of *fatum*.

It would be an oversimplification to consider all of Graeco-Roman culture as a direct extension of the belief in *fatum* since that culture, and particularly its philosophy, developed in profound conflict with the belief in *fatum*. But it was difficult to ignore *fatum*. Paul Ricœur pointed out that *fatum* was a symbol of evil, and evil accompanies men throughout their lives. The resistance to *fatum* was manifested in art, science, philosophy and politics. Almost every sphere of life was pervaded by an underlying urge to live in the light. The realm of *fatum* was darkness, and the man who could lighten that darkness could thereby avoid the ruses of *fatum*. The intellectual struggle against the power of *fatum* which was so prominent in Greek thought was later taken up in the Christian dialogue with the Greek tradition. Among the results of this dialogue are the Augustinian theory of free will, the love of God and grace.

Belief in *fatum* was the foundation of a particular concept of political power. The origin of power, its justification and its basic principle rested on *fatum*. Power only became power when it understood its actions as the fulfilment of *fatum*. Power did not need to take into account the desires of its subjects. Power was validated by the omens of oracles and by victories over enemies.

The irrational cult of cruelty is directly associated with the belief in *fatum*. This can be seen above all in ancient Rome where cruelty became an intrinsic component of art and entertainment. Cruelty was not a means to an end, but an end in itself. Its purpose was neither to compel confessions nor to inflict punishment for crimes committed. It had a qualitatively different function. Cruelty revealed the essential truth of the drama of life. *Fatum* was cruel. The cruelty revealed the ultimate truth of the lives of those from whom good fortune had turned away and those whom fate still favoured. Fate was like the gesture of Caesar in the amphitheatre: the upward or the downward motion of the thumb revealed the metaphysical depths of existence.

It would be an oversimplification to assume from this that paganism is only an historical and geographical category or an element in the culture of a given age. From the debate with paganism, it is clear that there is some ultimate, inexplicable, forever restless and rebellious internal element in human beings which begins to stir violently whenever the soul comes in contact with the word of God or with baptismal water. This element makes man unusually susceptible to the lures of paganism.

The link between modes of totalitarianism and pagan tradition is undeniable. Totalitarian ideologies are constantly striving to create and cultivate rituals. However ridiculous they seem to be to an outsider, their intention is clear. On closer investigation it became clear how deeply rooted they have been in Europe's pagan past. In totalitarianism, the belief in *fatum* is transformed into belief in the inevitability of the laws of economic and historical development. It is of secondary significance that these laws are ascribed to either race or class; the basic fact is that it is *fatum* that ordains some persons to live and others to die. The legitimation of power, according to these ideologies, is dependent on fate. The consent of the citizenry is deemed superfluous since it is sufficient to be in harmony with 'the objective laws of history'. Oracles have been supplanted by ideologists who claim to have a monopoly of insight into the objective laws of history. Victory over enemies confirms their ideological prophecies. According to Marxism, the ultimate criterion of truth is practice. But these victories are to a large extent matters of the interpretations made by the ideologists themselves. The unity of power and *fatum* reaches its height in the thesis that totalitarian power cannot be supplanted by any other power. If totalitarian power were to fail, the state would collapse; whole peoples and their world itself would go under.

The ideology of power has entailed an immense tolerance towards cruelty. Totalitarian power is cruel, and yet no rational justification for cruelty can be found in its ideological principles. The only possible explanation is the religious argument that the image of cruelty reveals the truth of the working of *fatum*: 'Such is life, and such is the fate of those who rebel against fate.'

Totalitarianism unites Jews and Christians in commonly experienced grief. For this common experience of grief to endure, it must build upon a deeper understanding of common faith. For ultimately, it is faith, and not just grief, on which a dialogue of understanding can be based. Otherwise, understanding would not last longer than the experience of shared grief.

The Levels of the Dispute

The confrontation with totalitarianism may take both practical and theoretical forms. The practical confrontation has involved the opposition and protest of individuals, who regardless of the consequences, have borne witness to their spiritual autonomy in a totalitarian world. Their protests swelled until the moment arrived when, in the words of Adam Michnik, 'different individuals who have become joined in opposition reach out to each other, linking hands in an invisible chain of good will, and in this way establish new social relationships. It is not true that despotic, totalitarian systems of government fall only as a result of external convulsions; often they evolve under internal pressure, and the course of this evolution is a fascinating phase on the road to freedom.'[2]

The theoretical confrontation aims at depriving totalitarianism of its ideological legitimation. Among the many intellectual opponents of totalitarianism, philosophy, which has religious overtones, has acquired a special significance. This is because totalitarianism inevitably seeks a sacral legitimation. This can be seen in the war which totalitarianism has waged against religion. After all, religion contains the idea of the sacred, in particular the idea of the sacred as the highest good. The religiously oriented philosophical criticism of totalitarianism has brought out the autonomy and authenticity of the sacred. This concern for authenticity should likewise pervade the criticism conducted on other levels. If totalitarianism seeks legitimation through ontology and related intellectual activities, then the confrontation with totalitarianism will restore the authenticity of these fields. The same applies to ethics, indeed the more so, since any deformation of ethics leads to catastrophic consequences for society. The critique of totalitarian power will show that totalitarian power bases itself on an erroneous conception of itself. Totalitarian power and its self-consciousness cannot stand up under serious criticism.

Confrontation at the Ontological Level

The ontological confrontation with totalitarianism postulates a protest against ontology's claim to universalism. The positive aspect of this dispute is the vindication of dialogue as an autonomous pattern of relationships of individuals. The fundamental issue is whether dialogue is indeed an autonomous pattern of relationships among individual persons or whether it is a derivative and in part illusory connection which obscures the more fundamental levels of a causal chain. The question is put more succinctly in the language of the Stalinist ideology: 'Is dialogue nothing more than a superstructure of the dialectics of nature?' or in the language of Greek drama: 'Is dialogue nothing more than a multi-voiced soliloquy conducted by *fatum*?'

An especially strong protest against the claims put forward for ontology has been expressed recently by Emanuel Levinas. He writes:

Political totalitarianism is based on ontological totalitarianism. Being is everything. Being, in which nothing begins and nothing ends. Nothing opposes it, no one judges it. An anonymous neutrality, an impersonal universality, a universe without language. Speech is impossible, for how else can the validity of the statement be confirmed if not by another statement, which no one will risk making.

The entire West recognizes itself in this wordless world. It has been proceeding from Socrates to Hegel in the direction of an ideal of speech in which the word has meaning only as a constituent of an eternal order which it brings to consciousness. At the end of this road, the person who speaks, feels that he is a participant of a conversation. The meaning of language does not depend on the intention which it contains but on the coherence of the conversation to which the speaker merely lends his lips and palate. Not only Marxism but also the whole of sociology and psychoanalysis provide evidence of language in which the crucial matter is found not in what the words say but in what they hide.[3]

There is now an increasingly large body of literature which upholds the autonomy of word and language. It presents detailed analyses of speech which has declined under totalitarian captivity, and of speech which is free, particularly that speech between God and man. Eugen Rosenstock-Huessy writes: 'The purpose of speech is to create peace, to express trust, to honour the aged, and to free future generations. The forms of speech must serve these purposes for without them all human speech decays. This has been so since the beginning of history. The power of human speech has always been at work.'[4]

I will not go into a detailed analysis of the concept of dialogue. I will only indicate some of its consequences.

The principle of dialogue above all recognizes the primacy of freedom over necessity. For before it becomes an exchange of words, dialogue is an exchange of free decisions. Whoever begins to speak makes a decision regarding whom he is addressing. Similarly the person addressed when he replies to a question has decided that he is in fact responding. God chose Abraham and called him by his name. Abraham responded to God's choice of him by the words: 'Here I am.' The case of Adam was different: when he was called by name, he ran off and hid himself from God. The principle of dialogue is freedom, and the extent of this freedom is symbolically revealed in the actions of Adam and Abraham. Levinas writes: 'The banal fact of conversation signifies that the system of violence has been annulled. This banal fact is a miracle of miracles.'[5] But freedom also implies that there can be world-views other than the world-view of those who exercise power. Dialogue puts the principle of totalitarian epistemology into question. It places the standpoint of power and that of its subjects on an equal footing; it rejects the claim of the powerful to be the sole interpreters of the mysterious intentions of *fatum*. Hegel drew attention to this in his analysis of the relationship between master and slave. The ascendancy of masters would cease if it were not recognized by the slaves. Subjugation is the result, not of the force of fate in history, but of the simple act of recognition on the part of the subjects. But such an act cannot be elicited by coercion. A person can be driven out of paradise, he can be forced into simulation, but he cannot be compelled to surrender in spirit if he does not want to surrender.

The principle of dialogue shakes the foundation of the totalitarian system. It happens sometimes that the word 'dialogue' is uttered by totalitarian power, and has happened particularly in recent times. In that case, the totalitarian power does not know what it is saying.

The principle of dialogue also has a great significance for Christian thought. It cautions against the temptation to yield to ontological claims particularly about the working of grace. The theology of grace is the core of Christian thought, for here thought impinges on the mystery of man's relationship to God. If the actions of God on man were the same as those of a totalitarian power, then there would be no protection from political totalitarianism. The attempt to understand the working of grace calls forth such a danger. It attempts to deal with the working of grace in the categories of stimulus and response. Cause and effect connect one being with another, one object with another. This connection does not entail consciousness or free will. Is grace a link in the chain of causality between God and man? Does God act on man without man's knowing it? For this to be so would require that grace be reduced to the categories of ontology and that 'grace' be a result of the working of fate. God's grace stands in contradistinction to the idea of *fatum*.

Sacrology

Sacrology, the study of the sacred, is the second level at which the confrontation takes place. The totalitarian interpretation of the sacred states that *sacrum*, as the supreme value, demands that everything, including the most precious values, be renounced. Summoned by the call of the sacred, the father sacrifices the son, and the son his father. The Bible presents this as the temptation of Abraham. Temptation makes the tempted person think that he is catching a glimpse of truth but not the full truth which is not accessible to him. A clear distinction must be drawn in the confrontation with totalitarianism between the sacred and the illusion of the sacred.

Totalitarian ideologies are not wholly incorrect when they say that the sacred makes claims to total submission. The sacred is the highest value to which human emotion can respond; it is a value which requires a certain unconditional acceptance. The first intimation of the sacred arouses in man the profound *trememendum* which then induces *fascinosum*. Between these two forces, man has no alternative but to yield. Such yielding by no means requires an acknowledgement of the metaphysics of envy. Such an acknowledgement causes man to sacrifice his son. The question however arises whether the ways of the living God can be reduced to influence over emotions.

Levinas once said: 'The *numinosum* or sacred enfolds man

and transports him beyond his powers and desires. But genuine freedom rejects such uncontrolled excesses. The *numinosum* nullifies the relationships between individuals by compelling them to participate, if only through ecstasy, in either a drama for which they have no desire, or an order which plunges them into an abyss. This, in some respect, sacramental power of the divine appeals to Judaism as a power which curtails the freedom of the human being and is contrary to an education of man which is an action based on freedom. It is not that freedom is an end in itself, but it is the prerequisite of every value that man can attain. *Sacrum* which enfolds and transports me is violence.'[6]

Rosenzweig in *The Star of Redemption* draws attention to an important phenomenon: the closer that Graeco-Roman paganism came to its demise, the more eagerly it increased and elaborated its *sacrum*. In the end, the pagan *sacrum* was ubiquitous: in every glade, village and house. But at the moment when God spoke, this *sacrum* disappeared and the world shrank to its normal dimensions.

The sacred arouses trembling and fascination but it cannot arouse what is most fundamental, namely the consciousness of responsibility. This, however, occurs at a completely different level from the level of the emotions. Every encounter with God arouses in us a consciousness of responsibility. Levinas writes: 'To know God is to know what must be done.'

The prerequisite for the emergence of the consciousness of responsibility, as well as its source and justification, is the presence of the Good. Man experiences the absolute Good in his encounter with God. The infinitely Good transcends the *sacrum* and is not attained through the emotions. The mystery of the influence of the Good, unlike other values, lies in the fact that whoever has encountered the Good wishes to do good, and does so selflessly. This selflessness banishes envy, and thereby the conflict between the supreme value and the value of what is closest to us disappears. Through the highest Good which is God, man acts towards his neighbour in accordance with the Good, which is the value closest to him. This brings that value even closer: the father draws nearer to the son, and the son to the father. The commandment to love one's neighbour is founded on this encounter with the Good.

Recognition of the absolute primacy of the experience of the Good in the triangular relationship between God, man and neighbour opens up a perspective, a new conception of power. God is the real ruler of man; God exercises his dominion through the Good. The Good closest to man is his neighbour. In a society which acknowledges God and which pursues the Good, ruling means serving.

Ethics

Ethics is the third level of the confrontation. The two totalitarianisms discussed postulated an ethical revolution as the prerequisite for the political revolution which they brought about. The old ethics were, according to them, to yield to the new. The old ethic was taken to mean the religious ethic derived from the Bible. The new ethic was to be based on the fundamental principle that the higher the value, the more justified the use of violence in its name. The antithesis to this would be that the higher the value, the greater the freedom. The basic issue is that of violence and the ethical limits of the use of violence.

The thesis that the hierarchy of values is not parallel to the hierarchy of the degree of violence to be applied has been accepted in ethical thought from Kant to Hegel and up to Scheler and his successors. Only the lower values connected with desires and basic needs put man under pressure. Values of a higher order such as justice, peace and the pursuit of truth flourish only in freedom. Their realization is conditional on their being freely chosen. What is important is not only the fact of certain axiological structures being established among men, but rather the fact that men themselves become the bearers of these values and embody them in their actions.

There can be no justice without just men, no peace without peace-loving men, and no pursuit of truth without devotion to truth. The outward realization of values must be a concomitant of their realization within men themselves. The internal establishment of values cannot be realized without freedom.

The issue of the ethical limits of the use of violence is essentially that of the underlying ethical experience in the course of which those limits are encountered. The purpose here is neither to promulgate yet another theory nor to offer an interpretation of commandments known for millennia. Both totalitarian ideologies have done this to serve their own ends. What we must do is to analyze an experience which would be prior to or presupposed by any or every theory. But is there such experience?

Levinas says that fundamental to ethics is the 'experience' of another human being directly perceived through his 'face'. This is not a superficial experience; it is something which transcends ordinary knowledge. He writes: 'Perception reveals names, and thereby classifies. Perception takes its object. It takes control of it. Possession denies the autonomy of being, although it does not destroy it; it denies and maintains it. A face cannot be violated; those eyes which are utterly defenceless and which are the most naked part of the body, offer absolute resistance to possession. It offers an absolute resistance and a readiness for martyrdom which is a temptation to murder; it arouses the temptation of absolute negation. To see a face is to hear "You will not kill." And to hear "You will not kill" is to hear "social justice". And everything that I can hear from God and directed to God who is invisible should reach me through this one unique voice.'[7]

The ethical experience described by Levinas is inherently tragic. That tragic element becomes resistance when it is associated with pangs of conscience and these set in, unfortunately, after the crime has been committed. The horror of murder is revealed only after the event. The value of justice can only be perceived in an unjust world. Cruelty gives rise to the need for mercy. This does not contradict what we have been saying. The memory of ethical catastrophes points the way to a better future. Levinas's reflections which are imprinted with the recollection of the Holocaust provide the point of departure for new hope.

Response to the Challenge

The intellectual confrontation with totalitarianism is primarily a dispute over the nature of power. Totalitarian power is pathological power. Observation of disease can permit a better understanding of the nature of health. It provides a clearer definition of our responsibilities in the face of the threat posed by totalitarianism.

Let us repeat our main observations: totalitarian power is directed at the subjugation of the whole man, and to this end, it has created a corresponding ideology to justify its actions. This ideology claims that power is the expression of the force which rules the world and the course of history. But there is a contradiction in this pursuit of man's total subjugation. Pursuit of total power over all things abolishes the distinction between ruler and subject. The abolition of the stratum of subject destroys the foundation of totalitarian power. In order to avoid self-destruction, totalitarian power which is aware of this must, therefore, constantly call into being new enemies. In order to exist, totalitarian power needs enemies as much as it needs subjects. Stalin saw this clearly when he formulated his celebrated theory that class conflict increases as Communism advances. The disease of totalitarian power originates in this contradiction. Totalitarian power creates enemies in order to fight against them; it fights against them in order to create them anew. Thereby, it exhausts all its creative capacities.

The Bible reveals totalitarianism as one of the greatest temptations to which man can be exposed. The thought that violence should be used for the good of man is very attractive; totalitarianism builds on this idea. Was it really not an honour for Isaac to be sacrificed to God? The temptation of totalitarianism should be taken seriously. There are many impulses in man which dispose him to yield to temptation.

This is all the more reason for those who know the Bible to remain vigilant. It is not only a matter of preventing the distortion of ontology, sacrology and ethics, and to protect man from the temptations which are made more attractive to human beings who suffer from the anxieties which are inherent in human life. It is necessary to provide a testimony of faith in the face of the extremes of life and death. Faith is the only force which can master the temptation of totalitarianism. The sources of faith are deeper than the claims of totalitarianism. The totalitarian temptation must recede before the far greater force of faith which draws on very much deeper sources. Man is more perfect in his humanity through his rootedness in these deeper sources. In returning his son to Abraham, God desired Abraham to gain in his humanity. Man realizes the humanity in himself when he makes a choice, and in his choice chooses the One who first chose him. He is himself when he remains faithful to the decision he has made. He is himself when he gives his word and accepts the word. Faith is fidelity to God and man. Faith brings out, from the depths of man into the light of day, the very forces which are decisive for his existence, namely, freedom, the word and fidelity.

In opposition to totalitarian power stands the human being who has been brought into being by faith. It is an exceptional person who breaks out of every category of totalitarian ideology. He entirely evades its grasp. Totalitarian power has no place for such a human being in its calculations. He should not exist, according to totalitarianism, but he does exist nonetheless. He should not speak but, nevertheless, his voice is heard. He should be frightened, but he is perfectly serene. This man should not be regarded simply as an enemy of totalitarianism, because if that were so he would be one with its agents and would be on their level, he is also not a supporter of the system. He transcends the totalitarian system and that makes him a great danger to it. He is the symbolic equivalent to a fortress which cannot be taken. His existence demonstrates the reality of a world which is utterly beyond totalitarianism. The ultimate aim of the dialogue between Judaism and Christianity that is now in process, following the experiences of the Holocaust, is a joint effort to foster the existence of human beings of such faith and bearing.

Translated from the Polish by Anna Pomian

NOTES

[1] J.Stalin, *Problems of Leninism*, Moscow, 1954, p. 713.
[2] A.Michnik, *Polskie pytanie [Polish Questions]*, Zeszyty Literackie (ed.), Paris, 1987, p. 131.
[3] E.Levinas, *Difficile liberté*, A.Michel (ed.), Paris, 1976, p. 267.
[4] E.Rosenstock-Huessy, *Die Sprache des Menschengeschlechtes* 2, Heidelberg, 1964, p. 478.
[5] E.Levinas, *op. cit.*, p. 21.
[6] E.Levinas, *op. cit.*, p. 29.
[7] E.Levinas, *op. cit.*, p. 22.

III

RELIGIOUS PLURALISM
AND CIVIL SOCIETY

Relations between Jews and Christians in Civil and Persecuting Societies

OWEN CHADWICK

One difficulty when comparing Jews and Christians in a civil society with Jews and Christians in a persecuting society is that the difference is sometimes smaller than might be expected. That is, the lines between a civil society and a persecuting society are unfortunately less clear than an idealist might wish. A constitutional state gives or may give – may give because the gift does not appear to be inherent in constitutions – guarantees of equal rights to all its citizens. Certainly constitutional states are the best means of preserving that equality in rights, but minorities can be persecuted by majorities even in the most constitutional of states.

It usually depends on whether the state is in crisis or not; if it is not in crisis, whether the citizens, or many of them, imagine that it is in crisis and are afraid of the unknown; or, if not so many of the citizens are panicky, whether a government for its own purposes can create a feeling of crisis which is then taken to justify injustice to a minority. In the summer of 1940 the British government was afraid. It was not only the government; otherwise sensible holders of chairs in universities drove out in their cars into the country and poked behind hedges to see if the brushwood concealed a spy. Thus they treated a lot of people unconstitutionally – among them a lot of exceedingly pro-British refugees who were exiles from Hitler's Germany but happened to have a

German name, German origins and spoke English with a German accent. The fact that a lot of them were Jews made no difference, for better or for worse, to the injustice with which they were treated by a constitutional state in panic.

In February 1933, Germany was still more or less a constitutional state. But it was one where many of the people felt that the crisis in the state was so dire that the cure of it must need drastic measures; and then someone obliged the government by burning down the Reichstag and converted the crisis into an obsession that justified extreme measures and the fatal constitutional or pseudo-constitutional demolition of the German constitution.

Government Dependence on a Majority

The next thing is that any government, whether it is tyrannical, oligarchical or constitutional, from time to time helps itself in governing the majority of the population by being unjust to some minority in the population. After the fall of Louis Napoleon the French created a true modern democracy. In the last thirty five years before the First World War their government treated the French Catholics badly, on occasion outrageously, certainly unjustly. The reasons were various. They were a little fearful – they were persuaded that the French Catholics refused to accept the principles of democracy and therefore their existence or their power endangered the state. They could justify their fear by the behaviour of some of the French Catholic extremists, including the anti-Semitism over the Dreyfus case.

Anti-Semitic policies thus often have nothing to do with religion. The Poles in Poland after 1918 were only about 65% of the people, unlike Poland today. They had three big minorities – Ukrainians, Germans and Jews. They treated none of them equally. The need for the new Polish state to be very Polish was an overriding need, or seemed to be so.

Now it is not certain that the Jews in Poland before 1939 were treated worse than the Ukrainians in Poland. That is, it is not certain that when Christians treated Jews unjustly their reason was the difference between Christian and Jew in religion or race. It was (in part at least) even more basic to humanity. It was the difference between a majority inside a state and its minority or minorities.

There is no shortage of evidence for this distinction even among the Nazis. The Propaganda Ministry directive to German newspapers in January 1940 read: 'The attention of the press is drawn to the fact that articles dealing with Poland must express the instinctive revulsion of the German people against everything that is Polish ... It must be suggested to the reader that Gypsies, Jews and Poles ought to be treated on the same level.'[1] This is not anti-Semitism with a Christian background; it is just hate against various peoples who are different and one of them is the most deeply Catholic people in Europe. If you go to the Warthegau, the central part of Poland annexed by the Nazis, it is quite hard to distinguish between Arthur Greiser's policy to the Jews and his policy to the Poles; and even more telling, it is sometimes nearly as difficult to distinguish his policy to the Poles from his policy to Protestant Germans. It is well-known that the most anti-Semitic racists in Hitler's Germany were also the most anti-Christian of Nazis. And it is known that increasingly after 1937 that was true of Hitler himself, so that by the time the war came he saw that Christianity as but one form of a Jewish heresy and that when the time came after he had won the war it must also be destroyed.

In the nineteenth century Bruno Bauer was anti-Semitic. But he was also anti-Christian. He hated religion. Some of the most fierce anti-Semites were not Christians but people who had rejected their childhood religion.

Thus the first step in the business of getting justice to Jews in a Christian society, or since 1948 to Christians in a Jewish society, has nothing to do with resolving religious differences but with devising a constitution in which the equal rights of minorities are fully protected while not risking the dissolution of the state. We are not dealing with a fundamental difference of religion and religious prejudice, but in the simple fact that minorities exist in all states and what are we to do to create justice for them?

Fostering Prejudice in a Democracy

It appears to be the case that by hard-won and bitter experience we have learnt that the rights of the minority are better preserved in a democracy. The reasons for this are obvious. Equal political power for every individual gives the minority power – in theory, for no one has power by having the right to cast a single vote. But we also need to recognize that modern anti-Semitism in Christian states has sometimes been fostered, or at least let loose by, democratic systems. A political party achieves supremacy in a democracy by promising more bread. But sometimes it tries to achieve it by playing on the fears of the majority of the people: and sometimes the fears of the majority of the people include the fear, or merely the dislike of, a minority.

It is worth comparing two Christians who lived in Germany, the one in a civil society, more or less, and the other in a tyrannical society. It is instructive to see their respective fates; for they were both, in the most different ways possible but also in the most intimate ways, entangled with anti-Semitism: one in Bismarck's Germany, the other in Hitler's Germany.

Nineteenth-century German Anti-Semitism

Adolf Stoecker was the strangest phenomenon in German parliamentary politics in all the nineteenth century. And it was stranger still, after all that was to happen, that even after the Second World War German voices, 'good' German voices, anti-Nazi German voices, could be heard saying that now was the chance to put into practice his ideals. He came from a simple home of the artisan class which was devoutly Lutheran and deeply patriotic to the Prussian ideals of the state.

He came under the influence of religious revivalism, experienced a personal conversion, found a wife from a revivalist family, and in a way this future politician was to be a sort of revivalist all his life. He started off in a normal way; read theology at university, was ordained to a country parish and then to a town parish – that was in 1866, the year of the Prussian-Austrian war.

What suddenly gave him a bit of a name were articles in the church press at the time of the Franco-Prussian war; articles of the sort which we met in the Second World War and can read of during the First World War too, on both sides of the battle: the mingling of patriotism with an appeal to the Christian virtues of self-sacrifice, obedience, loyalty, like some Cato trying to recall the decadent Romans to the virtues which made the state of Rome great; the need to strengthen the nation through the deepening of its religious and moral commitment, and bring back the German virtues which are the inner strength of the society and state, and be reminded of our 'makers' like Luther or Schiller. Stoecker's record during the war, and especially as chaplain in the garrison town of Metz, got him chosen as chaplain to the king and court preacher in Berlin (1874).

In Berlin he had plenty of space and he knew what he wanted to do. He wanted to get rid of liberalism in the church, and was quite a demagogue in the way he attacked both the more extreme liberals and the moderates. To break the power of liberalism in the church was the platform for him of breaking the power of liberalism in the state and society. He was afraid, like so much of Prussia and especially of Christian Prussia, of the rising appeal of the Socialist party with its anti-church slogans. He believed that liberalism was the reason why the Social Democrats made progress, and he urged the Protestant churches to unite against the atheism of Social Democracy. In 1878 he founded a new political party in Berlin: the Christian-Social Workers' Party was its name, and it was a flop. In the election of 1878 it got hardly more than a thousand votes and it is extraordinary that after such a fiasco Stoecker could continue to have a political career. Yet three years later he had a seat in the Reichstag.

The fact was, he was an orator who could move masses of people; and the aims which he had – to undermine liberalism and destroy the Socialists – were very appealing to people who had no idea how they could get hold of the German working class. He really did believe in his cause – on deep religious grounds. He was not just a politician; he was also doing a lot of good in the church in the ordinary way of preaching and organizing. Whatever else he was doing he was making the churches more conscious of their duty to society and its ills, as well as to individual souls. Some churchmen valued him because he campaigned hard to secure more independence for the church from state control. Some churchmen valued him because he knew what he believed and had not the slightest interest in the problems of the theological schools. He believed that the church could only be a power within German society if it were free. When he spoke he was impossible to misunderstand. No one could doubt his sincerity even if they disliked what he said. He really did want to re-Christianize German society. Moreover, what he said was said at a time of economic crisis and social unsettlement. The situation had at least a faint parallel with the German Conservatives and industrialists of 1930 onwards when they thought that here in Hitler was an ultra-magnetic orator who could convince the working class of the value of Conservative ideals.

Such an orator could only be magnetic by means of slogans: of the traditional virtues; God and the people; down with liberalism, down with the anti-patriots, down with the Jews, as corrupters of the national virtues of Germany, or as behind the Liberal party, or as behind Socialist ideas. These slogans were to be used in re-awakening the Christian faith among the ordinary German workers. As early as 1879 he had realized that in his oratory the anti-Semitic slogans were the most powerful in moving the little Berlin shopkeeper in the direction which he wanted, of giving an evangelical tone to German life again.

Historians have tended to see this anti-Semitic campaign of Stoecker's as a triviality, or quaintness, quite apart from his real influence. That was how some of his own contemporaries saw it. And the fact that they saw it as a triviality is a sign, in one way, of the strength of a civil society; just as it was a sign of British democratic strength when during the 1930s young Cambridge University students could not be persuaded to believe that Sir Oswald Mosley and his Fascist party were anything but a ridiculous, though distasteful, triviality in national politics. But when for a short time we find even Bismarck tolerating the anti-Semitic campaign in his effort to counter the rise of Socialism, and when we know what was to happen very few decades later, we suddenly realize that civil society is only strong up to a certain point in these matters, a point which admittedly is unknown and unpredictable.

The idea of re-Christianizing society rested on a conviction that society was basically Christian even if it rejected the church. It needed recalling rather than converting; and it needed recalling because its natural or God-given state had been corrupted by influences which were neither German nor Christian. There was a 'foreign' spirit among the people. Stoecker had been inspired by the brotherhood among those who fought together in war, and it was this military sense of community or *Gemeinschaft*, with its friendships and self-sacrifice and loyalty, which was a hidden sort of model for the way a Christian civil society ought to be. The task was therefore possible. Underneath, the people really were Christian. Clear away the foreign influences and you would have a true Christian society which was what Germany was intended to be.

Once a Nasty Demagogic Campaign Gets Going it Feeds Upon Itself Nastily

The anti-Semitism started for Stoecker as just one element in his speeches. But it was received enthusiastically. And as he went on he came more and more to feel that the Jews stood for the foreign influences which he wished to eject from German life. He was beginning to misuse his pulpit. He had huge crowds and claimed to be preaching the Gospel to them. But what he was doing was corrupting the way the Gospel was presented, not to change their lives for the better, but to confirm them in some of their worst prejudices.

As liberal society stood firm, and as Bismarck dealt only in political methods of coping with society and not in emotion or in nationalism, he became the enemy for Stoecker; and in this sort of language an enemy was not just a man of different political opinions but a sort of anti-Christ. In December 1892 he and his group succeeded in getting a nationalist, *völkisch* as the Nazis were later to say, and even anti-Semitic tone into the Conservative party. But it was an oddity there, and looked it. Basically the true German Conservatives shared the liberal apprehensions about civil society. From 1892 onwards more and more of them came to regard this Christian revivalist Stoecker as an embarrassment, and even a distasteful embarrassment. It was rather as if the modern American Republicans, most of whom were not particularly religious and none of whom were particularly revivalist, hoped to gain a lot of help from revivalist preachers in the 'moral majority' and suddenly realized that they needed to play down this proffered assistance because it would be counter-productive in getting votes. It took the German Conservatives four years, but in 1896, which is amazingly late, they at last expelled him from the party. That was not quite the end of Stoecker. He remained a politician but always on the fringe, a sort of has-been whose word was still reported in the newspapers but who made no difference to what happened. He remained a revivalist preacher; but not so many preachers retain the influence they had right on into their late sixties, and he faded out before his death in 1909.

This career is, or ought to be, alarming to Christians who care about Judaism and care about humanity and above all care about Christianity. A *Rechtsstaat*, a civil society, is found to be best met in a democratic society provided that democratic society does not come under such calamitous pressures or threats of civil war that the central government gets too weak to protect minorities. Prussia and Germany of the 1880s had a mixed constitution, but it was undoubtedly a *Rechtsstaat* with strong democratic features and, incidentally, a noble tradition of justice. In the eighteenth, and especially in the nineteenth, century that tradition had done a great deal for justice for the Jewish people of all Europe. It had also been built up very markedly by Jewish minds.

Since the days of Cleon in ancient Athens the world has known that a democracy is also compatible with demagogy, and that a triumphant demagogy is hardly compatible with democracy and is not compatible for long with a society of constitutional liberties: in the greatest democracy in the world we only have to remember the name of Senator MacCarthy. A democratic society does not have to be in desperate trouble, like the desperate German trouble of 1923, in order to start listening to demagogues.

In the Nazi years, one of Stoecker's former colleagues published reminiscences of him called *Prophet of the Third Reich* (Paul Le Seur, *Adolf Stoecker, der Prophet des Dritten Reiches*, Berlin 1936). At first sight this book was an attempt to revive the reputation of Stoecker by pointing to his *völkische* demagogy and his Christian-Socialism and his anti-Semitism. The book does this. But if the book is read with care it does something else. His programme is said to include the diminution of the number of Jewish judges to the percentage of Jews in the population; and the removal of Jewish teachers from national schools. But Stoecker is also said to be far away from *Rassenantisemitismus*. He is quoted thus: 'I don't fight Jewish people but their bad influence on German life; I don't fight Jewish faith but atheism which in press and public meetings attacks our Church poisonously.' It is pointed out that Stoecker was a strong defender of the Old Testament as God's Word. The book declares that it is very wrong to attack or to doubt the baptism of Jews. It says that to make

Christ an Aryan is a piece of scientific childishness which must discredit anti-Semitism among educated people. To such stupidities lead the errors of *Rassenantisemitismus*. In this way it can destroy the whole movement against Judaism (see Le Seur, pp. 20–23). The Jews must not be hated as individuals and condemned as people and fought as a race; in spite of the struggle against their dangerous destructive activity in society they must be seen as brothers in the great family of peoples, valued as erstwhile witnesses to God's revelation, and loved as fellow-citizens, even if under the command: 'Love your enemies.' That was all quoted out of Stoecker. Thus Le Seur's object in the mid-thirties was not only to commemorate Stoecker but to deprive the more extreme racial anti-Semites of the benefit of his name by putting forward less un-Christian elements in his language.[2]

An Anti-Nazi Pro-Jewish Russian Patriot

No one can deny, after the experience of more than two centuries, that revivalist preaching is a genuine and sometimes even inspired way of bringing ordinary men and women to decisions about religious truth or about a life of better quality. And yet we also find in history moments when religious revivalism and political demagogy go hand in hand and end in vile injustice, the most recent example being the rise to power of the Ayatollah Khomeini.

Now I take a Christian in a repressive society: Jochen Klepper. He was the son of a Pietist family in East Germany, but his mother had been a Catholic educated in a nunnery and came over to Protestantism on her marriage. That combination must have helped to develop the unusual religious quality in the son. He was a witness of mob-hatred of 'Reds' and Jews, as it was said, during the Kapp Putsch of 1920. He read theology at university and wrote a thesis on the early German Pietists, Francke and Gottfried Arnold. He did not know quite whether to become a journalist or a writer or a pastor or a theologian, and by the middle of the 1920s was writing for the theatre as well as for evangelical journals. At the heart of it was the call to resignation in the midst of suffering. He joined the Association of Religious Socialists, which also meant membership of the Social Democratic party. But mostly he was writing on art, and fashion, and broadcasting; for now he lived in Breslau in the house of a Jewish widow thirteen years older than himself, who was a fashion designer and had two young daughters. She was a totally assimilated Jew. He finally married her at a registry office in 1931. Both the German nationalists and the Nazi press began to attack this publicist for being a Judaizing Socialist.

The family moved to Berlin. There he found that he could not get his chance of publication or broadcasting so long as he was a Social-Democrat; and in 1932 he cut the links with the Social Democratic party and the Religious Socialists, so it cannot have been a very profound or principled socialism. Indeed he felt in 1932 that Heinrich Brüning, who was anything but a Socialist, had as Chancellor the best chance of saving German society. When Hitler came to power Klepper did not mind Hitler's nationalist ideals. But Klepper could not go with the Nazis, first because of what they were doing to the church, and secondly, and especially, because of the ever-increasing number of anti-Semitic acts. This feeling was, so to speak, not two feelings but one and the same. Of course it mattered that he was married to a Jew. But as a Christian, with a Christian sense of vocation, he saw the Jewish religious tradition as that which gave the Christians their world-mission. And as a Christian he was shocked by the silence of the church authorities over the anti-Semitic violence and screeching of April and May 1933.

He was sacked from broadcasting because he was denounced as a former Social Democrat who was married to a Jew. He began to write again. The most extraordinary episode of his career was that he now wrote a life of Frederick William I, and he turned this very unpromising subject into a tract about the way a powerful state protects true religion, and how the limits of power come when the proper God-given order of the state is trampled on and when the freedom of religion is destroyed. He was dedicated to the doctrine of justification by faith alone, and also to the Lutheran doctrine of obedience to the state, and never considered the possibility that it was his duty to resist the Nazi state. He happily pledged loyalty to the Third Reich, which was a condition of his continuing to publish. He played no part in the Confessional church, though he evidently respected Helmut Gollwitzer. But the Lutheran tradition was of ever more importance to him personally. He now started the idea of writing a biography of Katharina von Bora, Luther's wife, evidently because he wanted to portray the first marriage of a modern pastor and, we may guess, because he had a wish to reconcile himself intellectually to his own home and ancestry.

In 1937 the historical novel about Frederick William was published under the title *Der Vater* ('Father') and pleased the army and some of the government, and gave him a name that allowed him much more scope for writing. It was very curious. He looked and wrote like a German Conservative and nationalist, for whom the old Hohenzollern monarchy, the old traditions, the old faith and the old heroes, were the best hope and needed to be revived. Yet we know both from his wife and his past that this was far from representing his deepest thoughts. And yet this complicated soul is impossible to accuse, very seriously, of writing what he wrote for the sake of pleasing government and earning a living. In 1937–8, he really was a popular Christian poet and writer.

He was beginning, however, to be disturbed by the apparent indifference among his contemporaries, even those in the churches, to the persecution of the Jews. He was in fact curiously insensitive about it himself. He saw no future for the Jews – why did they not accept conversion to Christianity? He had no use for plans to emigrate; though his own elder step-daughter emigrated to England. The 'Crystal Night', and the terrible fate of many Jews including a few of his friends, finally brought home to him the agony and the danger facing his own wife and second step-daughter. On 18 December his wife was at last baptized, and they were married in church.

When the war broke out everything at first was fine for them both. Other Jews had to sell their property and be expelled to Poland for compulsory work. But he went on writing, and the army still recommended reading his book on Frederick William I, friends brought them rations because she and her daughter had no ration-book for clothes and had smaller rations of food than other people. Still, how long could it go on? They went to church together, and held concerts, and invited people to dinner; writers and artists and musicians and pastors kept asking them out. In the church at Steglitz he heard with emotion his hymn on the memory of the heroic dead. He thought of writing a patriotic cantata and of making a film about Prussian greatness, but he did not because he saw that the Nazis could use them. He wanted to win the war. He still thought that the victory of the German armies over liberal democracy would be like a judgement of God on the nations and could reopen the possibility of a restoration of a Christian Europe. If he were called up for military service, as he expected, he was very ready to go – indeed he wanted to go. He thought that in a war a human being must share the experience of war and not just get through it as a civilian. He still had the hope that the true German tradition as he conceived it, the Prussian virtues which were Christian virtues, would triumph in the end in Germany.

And yet the pair seemed to live on the edge of a precipice. He began to blame the Confessional church leaders because they did nothing for the Jews in Poland, whence the news came of terrible conditions. He did nothing himself. At a party, Kathe Staritz a Christian friend who was an agent of the Christian service trying to get Jews out of the country, the bureau run by Pastor Grüber, urged them to get in touch with Grüber at once. They did nothing of the sort.

In December 1940 he was called up and soon found himself in a supply unit in the Masurian Lakes. He went through the Balkan campaign into Romania with his unit. He heard that his patriotic book on Frederick William I was being reprinted with a very large print-run of 85,000, and that at a time of paper shortage. This individualist and aesthete drew inspiration from the close community life of the army, the camaraderie which he had never before experienced. He wrote war poems to celebrate it. There is no hint anywhere that he doubted the rightness of what he was doing or of what the army was doing, hardly a hint that he doubted the moral right of the government of Germany. He believed the war to be a 'just war'. He was proud of the victory of German arms and glad that a Hohenzollern prince fell in battle, because then the great name was linked with victory; but also he prayed earnestly that Hitler might have a change of heart towards the churches and the Jews. He thought that the victory in the West was God's will and prepared the way for a restoration of Christian Europe. It seems to have been the happiest time of his life. He crossed the border into Russia with his unit only a few days after the Barbarossa invasion started in June 1941. He loved the thrill of being part of a mighty advancing army.

All this was shattered three months later when he was sent home as not worthy to fight in the army because he was married to a Jewess. He knew that he was back on the edge of the precipice. Now he saw clearly what was happening to the churches, and what was happening to the incurables, and what was happening to the Jews. He turned for help to the Bible, and began to toy with the idea of suicide. He applied to the authorities that his step-daughter (at least) might emigrate to Switzerland or Sweden but was not surprised when she was made a worker in a Siemens factory though still under the menace of deportation to Poland.

The Minister of the Interior Frick much admired *Der Vater*, and often gave copies of it away. He saw Klepper personally and advised him to apply for readmission to the army and then the question of the visa for the girl to emigrate would be put to Hitler. But he told Klepper that the girl was in no danger of deportation. He gave Klepper a letter of protection for her.

Meanwhile the news of Jewish suicides kept coming in. Letters which he wrote to members of his wife's family came back marked 'Moved to Poland'. The big event for him was the suicide of a non-Jew, an actor, with a Jewish wife and their son. He was not sleeping and was in growing mental turmoil. He went to consult a clairvoyant or soothsayer and knew as he did so that he was guilty of superstition. He was still totally resigned, or totally passive, in his attitude to the state.

Religious Resignation in Tyranny

The most illuminating moment of Klepper's whole career, for our purposes, was the affair of his friend Kathe Staritz, whom we have already met as part of the Grüber bureau for helping Jews to get out of the country. With expert knowledge about what was happening, and unable to bear the knowledge without doing something about it, Kathe Staritz called on the members of her office to help Jewish Christians more decisively. Notice that she called on them to help Jewish Christians not just Jews. First the church authorities sacked her for her behaviour, though they kept on paying her. Then she was arrested and sent to the women's concentration camp at Ravensbrück. And the most illuminating moment of all was Klepper's reaction; the reaction of a Christian, married to a Jew, convinced that Jewish persecution was vile, in danger of losing his own wife and a beloved step-daughter. What he put in his diary still astonishes and disturbs. He blamed what he called her 'activism', her attempt to 'interfere with the leading of God'. When the Christian leaders of the Grüber Büro were imprisoned and sent to concentration camps, he condemned their efforts as 'activism'.

It is not God's way. It is not his will to make us confessors and martyrs. We have to learn that God can act without our help. Do we know what God is working in us, by laying on us at this time the need to keep silent? ... For us and anyone like us, the need of the moment is silence, endurance, waiting: and not hoping on the methods of this world. In the things of this world God can let us be destroyed; he has sometimes done that to the godliest of all. It is up to him how he works his will.

But Kathe Staritz was not a conspirator. She was not, absurdly, collecting stores of underground weapons or trying to influence some army officer towards tyrannicide. She was only trying to obey a law that one should try to love one's neighbour as oneself.

One is too much of a coward to act oneself; so one sublimates the cowardice and says that it is God's will and there is nothing we ought to do about it. Or put a little higher, one sees that nothing that one can do is the slightest good in these circumstances and if one does anything all one does is risk the life of a wife and a step-daughter; if nothing is any good, do nothing, and it must be God's will that one does nothing. But if someone takes the contrary opinion, that there may be situations where, morally, one ought to do something even when one knows that it is useless to try – if someone takes the contrary opinion and acts in a way which is bound to make him or her a confessor or martyr – then to blame them is almost unintelligible; or is intelligible only in the context of divinely ordered obedience to the state, even to a tyrannical state; and this obedience is part of one's faith. Did it make the slightest difference that this devout Christian layman was a lover of the Hohenzollern? I imagine not.

And might he have remained consistent in different circumstances? At one point there were secret discussions about whether they could get forged papers for his step-daughter and smuggle her over the Swiss border, by bribing someone they knew in the SS. Klepper gave no encouragement to this plan and talked of a 'pact with the underworld that is out of the question'.[3] Indeed that would have been playing with worldly methods. But it is hard to think that he would have vetoed the idea if someone else organized it and his step-daughter was willing to try.

It ought to be said that the attitude of the church authorities to Kathe Staritz was not much different. In June 1942, since she was in a concentration camp and therefore could not do her work, they stopped her pay.

Klepper had often and ferociously attacked the churches for not doing more for Jews and when they did more for Jews he thought it a wrongful effort to interfere with the will and the providence of God.

In December 1942 the Swedes said they would accept Reni the step-daughter. Now she needed a visa from the Security Service. Klepper went to see Eichmann himself. Eichmann sent a refusal next day. That night he committed suicide with his wife and step-daughter, believing that this was the will of God and doing the act in front of a picture of Christ. The church let them have a fully Christian service at the funeral.

Now, if this is the attitude of a devout layman – only one devout layman, let us not generalize – who does not only say there is nothing I can do, therefore I shall do nothing except say some prayers for the Jews, but actually says, anyone who does anything is behaving in an un-Christian way by using worldly methods – it is not easy to think that Christianity would have a powerful moral effect on some German boy baptized at home, taught elementary truths of Christianity at home, or school, or both, taken into the Hitler Youth, called up and put in the army, transferred to some *Einsatzgruppe* and told to shoot Jews because they are a danger to the state – in short, a Christian layman of a sort, but his Christianity, such as it is, is totally irrelevant to the matter in hand. He is much more likely to shrink from what he was told to do (thank God some of them did shrink from what they were told to do) by the emotions of compassion inherent in the human breast than because he was taught elementary truths about Christianity at school and was brought up in a society much influenced by a Christian past with a tradition of the *Rechtsstaat*.

Was Europe no longer a Christian Society and was the Question of Difference of Religion between Christians and Jews therefore Irrelevant?

Some people have suggested that the Holocaust proved that Europe was no longer a Christian society. But that statement seems to be a generalization without the slightest importance historically. This sort of evidence suggests worse things than that. It proves beyond all manner of doubt the weakness of religion – not just the weakness of religion but the moral weakness of religion – when confronted with the most powerful instincts of humanity like the instinct of self-preservation. People demand that the Pope should tell everyone not to be so cruel. Their demand is good. But the people who make it fancy not only that something can be achieved but that the Pope has the moral power to affect events. In the 1930s they did not see that, as one of the cardinals (Hinsley) said, the Pope was only a weak old gentleman inside the Vatican. He might have more armies than Stalin thought that he had. But the Holocaust proved that religion is not like that; not just the Christian religion, but religion. You can find illustrations to show the same moral weakness in the Jewish religion. What the Holocaust really suggests is something alarming to those who believe that religion is both innate in humanity and a force for the eliciting of the better moral instincts of humanity. It suggests something as formidable as this: there are civil societies and there are tyrannical societies, that is the fate of man, is how things happen, and religion is irrelevant to the whole question of whether demagogues or mutinous generals will get power and what they will do with their power. The damning thing is less Christian anti-Semitism than Christian failure to do anything; or, if that is too strong, to do much.

Let us put Opposite Axioms Side by Side

First, democracy is based upon some principles which can only be defended with a measure of religious sanction, principles utterly unprovable by reason, such as the rights of man or the equality of peoples. Therefore the Judaeo-Christian tradition has a fundamental place in the creation of civil societies seeking to ensure the reasonable freedom of the individual and justice for minorities. Secondly, it is agreed among the historians of Nazi Germany that the only ultimate philosophy of resistance to carry more than a few people was the resistance based upon certain religious axioms. The churches were weak as water but they stuck to two things which were incompatible with the Nazi world-view: that the Old Testament is central to the revelation of God, and that Jesus was a Jew and the source of rightful morality. Those two things do not sound like much in the game of politics, but they were enough eventually to alienate almost the entire leadership of the Nazi party from the churches. They were also enough to alienate all the more thoughtful Christian leadership from the Nazi party – though slowly, far too slowly, only really after the 'Crystal Night' of November 1938, and even then much more slowly than the hindsight of those of us who do not live under a reign of terror and a controlled press could wish. Thirdly, in retrospect the heroes of that age are religious leaders; Martin Niemöller, Dietrich Bonhoeffer, Maximilian Kolbe, Archbishop Sapieha of Cracow, Archbishop Saliège of Toulouse – though a lot of religious leaders were not at all heroic.

These three axioms are not enough to disprove the damning indictment by the Holocaust that religion does not matter in the least in the constitutional nature of a society. But they are enough to throw a doubt upon it. They are enough to make us refuse to accept it as a sweeping proposition without further reflection. Now let us consider their opposites:

First, humanity is divided in all sorts of ways by race, language, culture, class, dress and customs, but one of the most divisive forces is religion, as with Iraq–Iran, Palestine, Lebanon, Turkey–Greece, Northern Ireland, India–Pakistan, Sri Lanka, Serbia–Croatia, Tibet–China, and so on. Secondly, the division is usually racial at bottom, but the expression of it is quite often religious; as with the Protestant Irishman

Ian Paisley insulting the Pope at a recent Strasbourg Assembly, an affair where religion had little to do with what happened. Thirdly, the division does not usually lead to violence on religious grounds. But it can lead to massacre, as in the crusades on both sides, as with Hindus and Muslims during the partition of India, Turks and Armenians in 1915, Muslims and Christians in southern Sudan. The hostility was always basically racial or economic, or both. But in the state crisis and ensuing massacre it became utterly irrational and demonic, where a person of the other race was killed because he professed a different religion as much as because he belonged to a different race or spoke a different language. And all this because religious differences were the most prominent sign of the difference between the opponents, more public and more heartfelt even than the difference of language if such existed.

It starts to be possible to doubt whether rational considerations in the background really had the effect which is sometimes postulated for them. We are told that the racist theory of Gobineau, or of Houston Stuart Chamberlain, the scientific or pseudo-scientific theories of the social Darwinians, contributed in a big way to the development of modern anti-Semitism in Europe. But can they have done so really? It was the fine Jewish scholar Uriel Tal who said that Nazi anti-Semitism was a new thing, different from all previous anti-Semitisms – because it was irrational. He meant, I think, this. There was no longer any hint of such an argument as this: 'here are some people with some money let us take it and push them out.' There was no longer any hint in modern Europe of the argument of a barbarian world, that the Jews were blind and are blind to Christ when they have every chance of not being blind to Christ; they must be a wicked people.

The question has been asked whether the European tradition of anti-Semitism was the most important factor leading to the Holocaust. It is not denied by those who raise this question that it contributed. But they point out that in other countries and times anti-Semitism did not lead to genocide and that in other genocides the prime cause was not the difference of religion but the difference of race – though the difference of race was partly expressed and prominently expressed through the difference in religion. Even here, when we ask if there was any actual argument for the Holocaust we have to answer with a negative. Such arguments (or illogical absurdities with a vaguely rational veneer) are nothing whatever to do with the Holocaust. Klaus Scholder asked what the *goal* of the Final Solution was. And he answered his own question. It had no goal.

In this terrible conclusion religious men can take comfort from only two things. First, with regard to a civil society: it is agreed by historians that the Judaeo-Christian tradition of ideas and morality and conscience had something to do with the birth of democracy as an idea and the constitution of civil and just societies, even though the contribution it made will always be a matter of opinion; no reasonable historian is likely to deny this totally. Secondly, with regard to the tyrannical society: the moral resistance (moral as distinct from physical resistance) to what happened to the Jews among the Nazis was because of the basic recognition by Christians of their strong Jewish inheritance, inside their own inheritance a Jewish inheritance without which they could not themselves exist.

In 1988 I went to Venice. I happened to walk through the old Jewish quarter, the first ghetto ever, the quarter from which people were torn so murderously when the Republic of Salo came into being in 1943–4. The Republic of Salo was supposed to be governed by Mussolini. Actually it was governed by the SS and Italian thugs. The Italian people as a whole was not anti-Semitic and during the war, even while under pressure from the Nazis, treated their Jews, on the whole, well. The Catholic church defended Jews as well as it could in Fascist Italy. And yet, as I walked through the ghetto in 1988, I came across a service in the synagogue and found that the building had a little police guard. I asked one of the Italians why they were there. And he answered, 'It is still necessary.' Still necessary, after Salo! Only abuse, no doubt, from an odd hooligan or two, only graffiti perhaps – by looking about I found an anti-Semitic graffito – still necessary – and necessary in a constitutional state and a civil society.

Still, that is the elementary difference. In Venice of March 1988 the police were there to protect from ruffians, though there were no ruffians to be seen and they were not probable. Fifty years before, in Berlin of November 1938, the police stood by while the ruffians caused massive destruction. In what mood did they stand by? We can only guess. We can guess that there were various moods: 'there is nothing I can do'; 'there is nothing I am allowed to do'; 'how excellent that these people are getting their desserts'; and (we are allowed to hope) 'how vile that this is happening and that I cannot stop it.' How many felt like the last? We have no means of knowing. Perhaps it is better that we have not.

In Berlin in 1938, they stood, and watched, not to interfere. In Venice in 1988 they stood, and watched, in case they needed to interfere. This is no small difference.

NOTES

[1] *The German New Order in Poland*, London, 1942, translating documents from the Vatican, pp. 121–2.
[2] See the excellent essay on Stoecker by M. Greschat in *Gestalten der Kirchengeschichte* 9, 2 (1985), pp. 261–77; also G. Brakelmann, M. Greschat and W. Jochmann, *Protestantismus und Politik: Werk und Wirkung Adolf Stoeckers*, Hamburg, 1982.
[3] R. Thalmann, *Jochen Klepper. Ein Leben zwischen Idyllen und Katastrophen 1903–42* (1977), pp. 348, 361.

Religion in a Civil Society

ERNST-WOLFGANG BÖCKENFÖRDE

By civil society I mean not *any* political order but rather a *particular* kind. 'Civil society' does not mean exactly the same as 'state', but it is now regarded as the Western type of constitutional state. Its opposite is, in theory, repressive society. We are not concerned here with the general position of religion in and its significance for the political order of human societies as such; rather our subject is the position and significance of religion in a particular form of political order, the Western type of constitutional state, which is, or is becoming, predominant in the Western world.

Civil society is, among other things, distinguished by its recognition of human rights as the basic rights of individuals. This, the legal equality of citizens, and an effective realization of the principle of the separation of powers, is what makes it different from repressive society. Moreover, religious freedom is specifically one of these basic human rights. It is a legal principle which affects the form of civil society and is itself shaped by its status as legal principle *within* civil society.

By religious freedom I mean the right, within the state, to hold or not to hold a religious belief (freedom of belief); the right to profess or not to profess that belief (confessional freedom); the right openly to practise one's religion, or not (freedom of public worship); and the right to form religious communities (freedom of religious association).[1] This right is the right of the individual, as a human being and citizen, but it is also the right of the religious communities (for example, churches and sects) themselves. It is a right to individual and community freedom.

Religious freedom is, by its very nature, the right to a comprehensive range of freedoms. It includes on the one hand freedom of belief, profession of this faith, and open practice of the religion. On the other hand it is also the freedom not to have a faith, or to leave one's faith – in other words, to live without belief, profession and public religious practice. Thus religious freedom does not embody an assurance of the reality of religion, in the present and the future. It is only an assurance of the *possibility* of the present and future reality of religion.[2] Religion can be affirmed and cultivated in freedom, and it is on this freedom that its continued existence depends.

Religious freedom as a basic right of the individual is a public law which is part of the *ius civile*, the system of civil law. As such it is a law concerned with protection from the encroachments of other people and from the power of the state. It only relates to the human sphere; it does not deal with the relation of the human beings to God. It does not, therefore, free the individual from his moral duty to God to seek the truth and to espouse what he, in his faith, recognizes as truth, and to act accordingly. It does, however, prohibit other people or the power of the state from trying to impose their version of the truth.[3] Religious freedom exists as a public law not against truth, but for truth's sake, so that it can be sought and affirmed in freedom.

Religious freedom is nowadays also accepted by the Christian churches as a principle of public law. This has long been the case among the Reformed churches. The Catholic church, which has had the most trouble with this, has renounced previous positions, and, in the declaration of the Second Vatican Council on religious freedom – *declaratio de libertate religiosa* – has eloquently recognized this right, basing it on the dignity of the individual human being – *ipsa dignitate personae huma-*

nae. It has deepened this argument theologically on the basis of the freedom of the act of faith, which presupposes for its own sake the freedom not to believe.[4] Pope John Paul II has consistently followed this line of argument; time and again he has demanded the recognition of religious freedom as public law, which he sees as based on the nature and dignity of the individual human being. He asks for the church itself no rights and privileges beyond those which are derived from the principle of religious freedom itself.[5]

I see no difference in the position of the Jewish religion. Like Christianity, it is a dogmatic religion; it is convinced that the revelation at Sinai and the covenant with the people of Israel, with its promise of Israel's redemption, constitute the truth. But it does not therefore regard professing religion and being a member of the Jewish community as things which can be coerced or propagated by means of public law. It also regards religious freedom as among the rights to which human beings are entitled. To this extent there is present here, in my view, a common point of departure for Jews and Christians.

If religious freedom, as a basic right of the individual and of religious communities, belongs to the constituent principles of civil society, what consequences has this for the status of religion in such a civil society?

The Separation of the State from Religion as the Foundation of Religious Freedom

In a political order which recognizes religious freedom as a constituent principle religion is not fundamental to its existence. Religion as part of the political order was basic to the old concept of the *polis*, but the political order we are talking about now does not seek its legitimation in religion. Religion enjoys its freedom in this order; indeed it enjoys it through this order. It has the opportunity of developing in and from the conviction of its adherents, but it is not required for this political order. It is also no longer the common ground on which the state and the churches incontrovertibly stood, and which they invoked when they worked together or when they mediated conflicts. When this was so there was a basic assumption that the state was an all-embracing, self-sufficient '*societas perfecta*', with authority as the 'temporal power'. Civil society, as a secular temporal political order, departs from this pattern. It not only does this by allowing different confessions and religions to operate alongside each other. It goes further than this by declaring itself fundamentally neutral in matters of religion and philosophies of life (religious and philosophical neutrality). Where a state religion continues to exist formally as in some monarchies of the Western world (for example, in Great Britain, Sweden), the situation has become much the same in substance, apart from a few isolated areas where remnants of the old forms survive.[6]

This exclusion of religion from the jurisdiction and activity of the state, the renunciation of the long-prevailing religious supremacy of the state, requires a still more precise definition. It takes the form of a 'liberation' of religion; this liberation has a twofold character. First, it means the end of the institutional and practical connection between the state and religion. The state as such no longer 'has' or 'espouses' any religion. 'Religion is no longer the spirit of the state, it has become the spirit of civil society ... It is no longer the essence of society; it has become the essence of diversification,' as Karl Marx so aptly put it.[7] That is one side of the liberation. Another side is that religion is free to act positively in the spheres of individual and social freedom. Through the active convictions of citizens (as members of their respective religious communities), religion can without doubt achieve social and political significance. It is not simply confined to the private realm, nor does it as such lack a potentially public character. If it does acquire such importance, however, it must do so without being part of the necessary and indispensable practical institutions of the political order, which are determined not by any particular religion but rather by the earthly exigencies of the polity. Religion, the Christian as well as the Jewish, is thus not incorporated into the institutions of the political order. It has a real significance, but its significance is not given in the legal and normative obligations of the political order.

The Persistence of the Power of Civil Society to make Political Decisions dealing with Secular Purposes

The acknowledgement of religious freedom, and the renunciation by the state of its own sovereignty in matters of religion which that entails, has as a consequence that the political order restricts itself to secular affairs and purposes. Spiritual or religious ends lie outside its jurisdiction. This does not mean, however, that the state foreswears its comprehensive and potentially all-pervasive powers of regulation and adjudication. Rather this persists, little affected by being limited to secular purposes. Not everything that has to do with religion, or to which the religiously legitimated obligations of action and life apply, is excluded from the jurisdiction of the state.

As a matter of fact only the purely religious – the specifically 'spiritual' matters such as ritual, liturgy, worship – are excluded. The boundary between the 'spiritual' and the 'secular', or between the 'religious' and the 'political', is such that it is not determined primarily by matters and objects, but rather by ends or intentions. Everything is spiritual or religious which is aimed at the *salus animarum*, the eternal salvation of man; everything is secular or political if it concerns the earthly social life and welfare of human beings. As a result of this, there is a large area of what one might call *res mixtae*, which have at one and the same time both a spiritual and a secular aspect (marriage law, Sabbath observance and the performance of or objection to military service are a few examples). The political order claims the right to regulate all earthly matters, even when such matters also have a spiritual dimension when they are defined by a religious precept on how to live one's life. The political order insists, for the sake of public peace and its maintenance, on having the last, and decisive, word. This claim extends to all things which are relevant to the achievement and maintenance of public order. It also extends to all matters which are of importance for a just social order enabling people to live together in freedom. Consequently, there is no sphere of life, and no situation, which can be excluded *a priori* from having such significance.For every facet of human society – language and nationality, religion and customs, the distribution of property and the division of labour, relations between the sexes and the education of children – can be the object of dispute, conflict and tension.

This means, however, that even where religious freedom is acknowledged, as long as the religion in question does not limit itself to reverence for God through liturgy and worship alone, but also refers to life in the world, and adduces maxims on how to act therein such as the Ten Commandments, there remains the need for a compromise or reconciliation between secular and political ends and norms on the one hand, and spiritual and religious ends and norms on the other. The question remains as to how far religion, in its secular repercussions, can, or may, be accommodated in the social order fixed by the state; or, put in a weaker form, to what extent leading one's life according to religious principles can, indeed must, be allowed for in such an order. An area of co-operation, but also an area of conflict, between state and religion may well result from this. The problem is not solved merely by the acknowledgement of religious freedom and by the confining of the political order to secular matters; rather it only raises the problem.

The Autonomous and Free Activity of Religious Communities and Churches within Society and vis-à-vis the State

Even where religious freedom is acknowledged the relationship of religion with state and society must be defined. What does such a relationship look like, given the principle of religious freedom?

The first feature of the relationship is the autonomous and free activity of the religious community or the church. Religion is free when it can be practised without interference or regulation by the state, in the manner and organizational form which derive from the content of the religion itself. This is the basis of the autonomy of religious communities, and includes everything having to do with the internal affairs of the religious community: the organizational structure, the establishment of offices and appointments to them, the training of clergy, the fixation of the ritual and other forms of religious life, and the exposition and interpretation of doctrine. This autonomy is complemented – as a necessary corollary – by freedom of action. The limits of this freedom are defined first by the traditional spheres of the exercise of religion, such as preaching, divine service, religious instruction and religious philanthropy, (care of the ill, relief of the poor and so on). Distinct from these are further categories of religiously motivated activities within a secular sphere; the aim of these activities is to realize the religious way of life and the application of religion in the world. These activities are intertwined with secular, social, cultural and other activities, which may be regulated by the legal system of the state. Within this context of the legal system these are free and open, also, to realize religious principles and ends. They are not, however, part of the specific freedom of religious activities as such.

Autonomy and freedom of activity are aspects of the *status* of religion in the polity. They do not, and cannot, mean that the legal system of the state and the way of life of the society must necessarily be determined in their substance by religion.

Whether and to what extent that is so, depends on the *ordre publique* of the particular polity, and in what way the legal system and way of life of this polity have been formed by social and political factors. The autonomy and freedom of religious communities present opportunities, but only opportunities, to exert influence and have a determining effect on state and society. To what extent this in fact occurs depends on the convictions of the religious communities and their adherents, but it is also dependent on the existing political constellation. Precisely for this reason conflicts cannot be ruled out. Such conflicts may arise in almost all spheres of life; but they are not related to the status of religion and its activity as such; they only concern distinct matters in the field of legal order and order of life.

A second feature of the relationship between religious communities and the state and civil society is the balanced separation between the state and religious communities. The idea of the separation of the state from religious communities arose historically in the course of the polemical attack on the church, which was often allied to, even often overlapping with, the state. In reality, however, this idea of separation, when correctly understood, served not only the independence and autonomy of the state, but also that of the state *and* the religious communities.

The separation which concerns us here is not a one-sided one, which makes religion free from its dependence on the state. It has two sides, so that it helps to provide autonomy and independence for both the state and the religious communities in their relationships with each other, by breaking their organizational and institutional ties. Precisely because the two organizations have become separated from each other, each is able to act independently of the other, to perform its own tasks. The separation is not a radical one; rather it is balanced. As regards the religious communities, this balance consists in the fact that, while lacking any institutional voice or share in the power of the state, they are not in any way prevented from engaging freely in secular affairs of political and social order. Furthermore, the religious activity of believers, precisely because of religious freedom, does not lead to legal disadvantages for them. As far as the state is concerned this balance can be seen in the submission of the religious communities to the laws of the state – the freedom of these communities is itself provided for by those laws. The balance may also be seen in the fact that the rights and duties of the citizens are not dependent on religious affiliation, and finally in the refusal of the 'secular arm' to enforce the internal, belief-oriented demands which the religious communities make on their own members.

Fixing the Limits of the Position of Religion

The relationship of religion and the state is manifest in the autonomy and free activity of religion as well as the symmetrical separation of the state and the religious communities. This relationship does not, however, provide a way for the re-establishment of any institutional link between civil society and religion through a claim to this religious freedom. The exercise of religious freedom can indeed lead to the influence of religion on society and on the state, and on the formation of the legal system. The yeast of religious belief can, if it is strong enough, leaven the world. But this effective exercise of influence cannot raise any question about the foundation on which religious freedom and the symmetrical separation of church and state rest. Religious freedom as the principle which informs the relationship of state and religion, and the religious and philosophical neutrality of the state which is its complement, cannot be nullified by the claim to religious freedom. The fulfilment of the ostensibly religious principle that error as the opposite of truth has no right to exist, to be propagated or to be acted upon, provides no grounds for the abolition of religious freedom. It is not irrelevant to stress this limit, living as we do in the shadow of religious fundamentalism.

Thus far we have discussed the position of religion in a

civil society and the opportunities which arise in civil societies for religious communities. In the same way we must now ask what meaning and function religion has for civil society. Is it a matter of complete indifference whether one or several religions are active in a political community, or is this political community dependent possibly on religion, or on a particular religion, without being able to guarantee that religion's existence?

Definition of the Problem

What is the intellectual foundation of the state, the political community which embodies the necessary degree of unity (homogeneity), given the fact that religion is no longer obligatory – thanks to religious freedom – and so cannot perform this function? Can the state acquire this foundation naturally, perhaps from its political and cultural heritage, or through rational understanding, or through the active and deliberate consent of its citizens, or the satisfaction of the latter's social and material demands or 'interests'? Or is the state, as Hegel put it, suspended 'in the air', so that it requires a civil religion represented in propositions which claim for themselves unconditional validity?

In former times, religion was – at first in its embodiment in the institutional and legal system, later as a constituent in the collective consciousness of the whole society – always the strongest force for cohesion in the political order. The attitudes needed to sustain the state – the internal, self-regulating forces of freedom, of which, as a state founded on freedom, it had a special need – derived mainly from religious beliefs. Great political thinkers, from Machiavelli and Thomas Hobbes to Hegel and Alexis de Tocqueville, also insisted on the importance of religion as the foundation of the political order, even if this was done partly for 'Machiavellian' reasons, which attributed little intrinsic value to religion.

In the nineteenth century nationality, or national collective self-consciousness, was thought capable of providing the political and cultural identity needed for the cohesion of society. The nation was regarded as 'sacred' (in a secularized form), to the existence, honour and greatness of which it was even worth devoting one's life.[8] Zionism, as a specifically Jewish national idea, should also be included here. The idea of nationality itself draws on the spiritual and cultural heritage of the past. In contrast to the ideas of the individual and of the pluralistic society, which derive from the general principle of human rights, the idea of nationality has no distinctive substantive content. Moreover, with the political deformation it has suffered in the twentieth century, above all in Western and Central Europe, it has forfeited much of its formative power.

With this we see confirmed the thesis that the state of the present day, as a liberal and secular state – that is, as a civil society – rests on assumptions which it itself cannot demonstrate.[9] Despite the attainment of sovereignty, it is no longer a self-sufficient *societas perfecta*; on the contrary it depends for its own foundation and maintenance on other ideas and principles.

Against this background, it is understandable that efforts are made to assign to religion the functions of the maintenance of the political community. In a certain sense it is conceived as performing functions for the state and for society, as a kind of embodiment or transmitter of the 'value-consensus' which the state itself cannot create. Religion is expected to perform this function without the state's being bound in its own order by the substantive values which are contained in the religion. The end which is to be realized is that the state and society are amalgamated into a self-sufficient political community, secular and pluralistic. The question is, how far can religion and religious communities accept the performance of these functions for the political community? Is it consistent with their task and mission to perform these functions for the state and society and thus perform a service for humanity and its secular and political order? Or must they, for the sake of their own identity and mission, resist being pressed into such a service? Every religion, in my view, must answer this question for itself, according to the substance of its faith and mission. Otherwise it will act contrarily to its nature.

The Integrative and Legitimatory Functions

It is not rare to hear that religion performs an integrative and legitimatory function for the political community. This function appears in the process by which consensus is engendered and strengthened in society, and in which the ostensible consensus about values in society is transmitted and reproduced. A pluralistic and open political community, which is thereby a civil society, certainly needs a fundamental consensus to survive. It needs such a consensus to resist the centrifugal tendencies which result from philosophical, spiritual and ethical pluralism. Religions and religious communities are powers which generate fundamental ethical and moral conceptions and attitudes, and maintain them. This usually happens in a way which fosters community in society, to the extent that the religions and religious communities give support to the existing social order and the ethical and moral attitudes which prevail in it. Society is thus provided with a religious foundation.

As we have treated it so far, the effect which religion, or a religious community, has on society belongs in the category of empirical fact. Can any normative conclusions be drawn from this factual proposition: can we draw any conclusion from it about the task or mission of religion? If one regards religion on its own terms it does not appear that it has an obligation to contribute to the integration of pluralistic society by creating an appropriate consensus. This can, it is true, be a consequence, but not necessarily so. The cultivation of their own properly religious tasks might lead religious communities to speak and act in a way which has a disintegrative effect on society. They are after all obliged, for the sake of their identity and credibility, not to contribute to an order which may, admittedly, be based on liberal and democratic principles, but is no longer built on the basis of that which, to the religion, is indispensable. The fundamental consensus of a pluralistic society as such must after all have the support of the majority. Its basis is therefore not necessarily the lowest common denominator, but its support must nevertheless be very broad. Christian, as well as Jewish, teachings, in contrast, make a far-reaching claim which, in the practical context of secular society, can only be deliberately accepted and applied by a minority. This claim prevents both Christians and Jews from looking upon their religion as the integrative factor in society on the basis of, and within the limits set by, a fundamental consensus which can gain the adherence of the majority. To see their religion in this way and to act accordingly would be no different from passive adaptation.

The same is true with regard to the legitimatory function of religion. A religion, especially the Christian and Jewish religions, can without doubt contribute to the legitimation of the political order as such. It can heighten the loyalty, obedience and self-sacrifice of its members. This is a result of the fact that the Christian and Jewish faiths, on the basis of their own principles, affirm the social and political orders of the world, and summon the faithful to serve them. Notably it is not inherent in their nature to accept and advance the legitimation of existing political orders: this can only ever be a subsidiary consequence of religion and depends entirely on the extent to which the articles of faith are congruous with the recognition, or even the active affirmation, of the secular and political order. This is not however an affirmation in principle. The achievement of a balance between religion and the political order is itself a function of freedom. The influence of a religion on the political order is not confined to legitimation or integration. Religion can deny the legitimacy of the state. It can have a disintegrative effect where certain actions or institutions of a state or a society are found to be irreconcilable with fundamental religious obligations.

The Critical Function

This brings us to the question of whether, and to what extent, religion has a critical function to perform with regard to state and society. Such a question was not of central importance in earlier times, but during the last two decades it has come to take a prominent position in theology and in discussions within the churches. This is connected to the recent increase of interest in 'political' theology; it also has to do with the intellectual efforts to face the facts of the conduct of the churches during the Nazi era, and their attitudes towards dictatorial regimes, social injustice and exploitation in Western and, not least, in Latin American societies. The churches perform this critical function of religion by the uncurtailed advocacy of their own truth. The critical function is evident everywhere where the mission of religion is aimed at the individual human being, his calling and his dignity and at the relation of human beings to each other.

This is especially the case in the Christian and Jewish religions. Their message is about human beings and for human beings, not least through the crucial statement that the human being – every human being – is an image of God. It was in this sense that Pope John Paul II has said that the church, called to proclaim the truth made evident in Christ, can do no other than to join in the battle for that dignity which every human being attains in Christ, and can attain for all time. It 'must call injustice by its name, it must call by its name the exploitation of human beings by human beings, or the exploitation of human beings by the state, by institutions, by the machinery of the economic system ..., every act of violence against human beings, against their bodies, against their spirit, against their conscience or their convictions.'[10]

This critical function of religion is open to the danger, however, that it might result in religion becoming separated from the objective of the proclamation of its religious truth, and becoming instead a sort of independent, institutional source of criticism, which is no more than religiously motivated. With regard to the proclamation of religious truth criticism is not the proper objective at all, but rather only derivative from the unqualified proclamation of the religious message in its human dimension. The proclamation of religious truth as such does not aim to realize or oppose specific political or social orders and programmes. Critical statements about such systems and programmes should be made only in relation to religious truth and their bearing on the common life of human beings. Only when this is taken into consideration can the situation be avoided where religion, both Christian and Jewish, becomes a radically politicized force which threatens to tear apart any political order. This can happen when religion calls politically into question, with theological immediacy and unconditionality, the – eschatologically – provisional and fractured nature of such systems. This is characteristic of all impassioned 'enthusiasm'.

The critical positions which religion takes in relation to the state and society must be kept distinct from its role as pastor and guardian. The role of pastor and guardian is above all ascribed to the Christian churches. By this is meant the task of being something like an 'official conscience' in the political community. The role of guardian is supposed to be called on 'in acute situations, when the humanity of human beings, their human rights, are in such danger that keeping silent about this situation would be directly and immediately tantamount to the denial of Christianity'.[11] Included here are the basic preconditions of moral and legal order, the ethical minimum of the orderly living together of human beings. This role of pastor and guardian is not so much allowed to the churches today as demanded, for it is also in the interest of the political community.

At this point what is problematic in the role of pastor and guardian becomes evident. The readiness to acknowledge this role of the churches, or of religious forces in general, is an attempt on the one hand to use their public activity – or more precisely their public challenge – in the service of the political community. It is also an attempt to limit the scope of that challenge to the need of the political community for integration. Churches and religion are recognized and encouraged as the responsible organs of the ethical minima of civil society, whereby civil society relieves itself of the responsibility of dealing with this on its own. On the other hand, the legitimacy of such public challenge is confined to the maintenance of these ethical minima. If the challenge goes further than these ethical minima, it is criticized for transgressing the boundaries of this role as pastor and guardian.

The true basis of this misunderstanding is the assumption that it can be religion's task, and especially that of the churches, only to ensure certain minima. Their task and mission are to proclaim the truth which has become manifest in them in all its fullness; they are not there to confine themselves to the minimum, and only then to demand and exhort. The idea of the role of pastor and guardian is dangerous when the infringement of such limits might become the criterion and the limit of public challenge, out of consideration for religious and ecclesiastical responsibilities. These roles are to be understood as a function arising from the extensive and comprehensive mission which religion and churches have by their own nature. Does not the case where 'silence would be equivalent to the denial of faith' already exist when, for instance, the churches, instead of drawing from the fullness of revelation and thus (also) becoming a 'symbol of contradiction', are content with merely ensuring their survival?

In conclusion we should ask briefly in what ways religion can develop its influence in civil society. We should bear in mind here that religion appears and can be influential in the political and social order of civil society in two ways. First, religion takes the form of religious communities, which as institutions are represented by officials, and thus act collectively. Secondly, religion appears in the multiplicity of believing individuals, who live by their religion and attempt to give it reality in their lives, quite apart from their membership in corporately organized collectivities. These two forms have different modes of activity and influence.

The Influence of Religious Communities as Such

For religious communities as such – their institutional offices and officials – what is important is that they recognize their own calling, which their religious faith and its religious mission demands by its very nature. The calling lies in the proclamation of this mission, and the commitment to its truth. This is a spiritual and religious mission, not a political one. It is not concerned with the preservation or combatting of political orders and systems, or with being partisans in political disputes. All positions which a religious community takes must be in accord with its own mission.

However, inasmuch as a religious community proclaims its own mission in this way, espouses it for its sake and acts in its name, it necessarily has an influence on the life of human beings, and on their society. It does so because, and to the extent that, its message is at its core also a mission for human beings and of human beings. In this sense it has an inescapable political impact, in so far as it perceives its own task as being of this world and for this world.

This appears at first paradoxical. It becomes intelligible when it is made clear that 'the political' – contrary to a widespread view – is not a sphere on which one can impose boundaries, and which exists alongside or beneath the religious sphere. 'The political' is rather a public sphere of relations between human beings, individually and in collectivities, which is characterized by a certain degree of intensity of association and dissociation, and which occurs in, and has 'substantive objects' from all spheres of life (Carl Schmitt).[12] Thus even the religious mission of a religious community, which is, as such, purely spiritual, can repeatedly find itself, depending on the occasion, in the realm of political relationships and conflicts.

The guiding principle which the religious community

should follow when, through its officials and its institutional offices, it acts on society and in its relations with the state, can neither be the avoidance of the political in every case, for the sake of the 'purity' of the religious mission, nor the automatic commitment to a political attitude. Indeed, religious communities must, without wavering, be faithful to their own mission. Precisely in the unqualified commitment to this mission, free of short-term political calculations and contingencies, is the basis of political influence; this is what makes it possible for religion to bring into play its own standards with regard to the political realm. If the religious community finds itself, without wishing it, in the political realm – this can and does repeatedly occur – it must accept this situation and bear up under it. In this sense the guiding principle for the activities of religious communities is the exercise of 'apolitical political influence'. Although the starting point of religion is apolitical, and concerned only with the proclamation of its own message, it is potentially wholly political in its repercussions without this effect being sought or being set as an objective.

The Influence of the Faithful

The realization of religious beliefs in, and their translation into, the life of the state and society, in and into the world of politics, is nowadays largely a matter for individual believers – in ecclesiastical language the laity. The immediate field of action of the religious communities as such, and their officials, is in this respect limited, especially in a democratically organized political community. It is also primarily confined to the critical function of religion, and hence to the espousal of attitudes of contention. Positive influence on the organization of the legal system and of society and the state, and the realization of religious beliefs in the world which that entails, are nowadays primarily tasks for the believers as citizens of civil society. In a democratically organized political order this influence must be accomplished in and through

142

the democratic political process, not by trying to get around it. The religious community can make its views known by suggesting, encouraging, even going so far as warning against certain policies or actions; it can encourage the faithful and thereby prepare them to be active as citizens. Yet it cannot demand from those who exercise political authority the recognition before all else of its own principles and ideas of order. The realization of such principles and ideas of order, including those of natural law, requires, in a democratic order, that their spokesmen enter the political process in state and society and commit themselves to those principles and aims. There is hardly another situation in which the words of John Paul II are so well confirmed: 'The church is in the world through the laity.'

The central role which the individual believers have as citizens in realizing their religion in the secular political realm is now, as far as I can see, recognized by various religious communities. The Jewish religious community has no hierarchical organization which might control the actions of its adherents. In the same way there exists no such problem in the Protestant churches, because of their own understanding of office and hierarchy. The Second Vatican Council has emphasized the autonomy of the mission of the laity in the Catholic church too. Indeed it has even recognized the laity's qualification to take part in Christ's office of priest and prophet.[13]

John Paul II has expanded and deepened this view of the Council yet further: 'It is their [the laity's] specific vocation and mission to express the Gospel in their lives, and thereby to insert the Gospel as a leaven into the reality of the world in which they live and work. The great forces which shape the world – politics, the mass media, science, technology, culture, education, industry and work – are precisely the areas where lay people are specially competent to exercise their mission. If these forces are guided by people who are true disciples of Christ and who are, at the same time, fully competent in the relevant secular knowledge and skill, then indeed will the world be transformed from within by Christ's redeeming power.'[14] The task of believers, and its autonomous nature, could hardly receive a clearer or more fitting formulation. There is no longer any place for dominance by the officers of the church, bishops as well as priests, over the laity in the recognition of this, their mission.

Translated from the German by Steven Beller

NOTES

[1] On these individual rights, which are the constituent parts of religious freedom, and which were realized historically only in a sequence of stages, see G. Anschütz, 'Religionsfreiheit', in Anschütz/Thoma (eds), *Handbuch des deutschen Staatsrechts* 2, 1932, pp. 675–89.

[2] See E.-W. Böckenförde, 'Das Bild vom Menschen in der heutigen Rechtsordnung', in Michalski (ed.), *Der Mensch in den modernen Wissenschaften. Castelgandolfo-Gespräche 1983*, Stuttgart, 1985, pp. 91–100 (93).

[3] E.-W. Böckenförde, 'Religionsfreiheit im Spannungsfeld zwischen Kirche und Staat', in *Schriften zu Staat, Gesellschaft, Kirche*, Bd 3: *Religionsfreiheit: Die Kirche in der modernen Welt*, Freiburg, 1990, pp. 32–57.

[4] Second Vatican Council, *Declaratio de libertate religiosa: Dignitatis humanae*, cap. 2.

[5] See *Encyclica Redemptor Hominis*, no. 17; address to the General Assembly of the UN on 2 October 1979. Published in German in *Osservatore Romano* (German edn), 5 October 1979, p. 10.

[6] In the discussion at our conference in Vienna a Jewish participant made the objection that the concept of religion employed here was Western. For Jews, he claimed, religion means something different from what it did for Christians. To be Jewish included membership in a community which was formed by its affinity with a particular territory and a culture as well. Thus 'to live in Israel' was in itself a religious concept, and religious symbols and concepts were indispensable in a Jewish state. Once, however, civil society included religious values, and could not exclude them, the right also had to be granted to realize one's own interpretation of what is Jewish, and the political order had to be arranged accordingly. In doing so, of course, religious liberty for Christians and Muslims would be guaranteed.

This objection results from a particular conception of religion; it is one which sees religion – as in antiquity – as the religion of a *polis*, the religion of a concrete people, which is politically organized. Religion from this point of view is part of a religious and political primordial community, which is inseparable from that religion. This conception of religion may be close to the Jewish tradition. The God of Abraham, Isaac and Jacob reveals Himself as the God of the people of Israel, and the covenant is as such one with the people of Israel. The Christian religion is, by comparison, explicitly a religion for all humanity. It is there for each and every human being, not for one particular people or peoples as a part of their primordial community.

The question we must ask is to what extent the basic order of civil society can coexist with a religion of the *polis* whose ultimate reference is a religious and political community. Or does civil society tacitly assume a universalistic religion, such as is embodied in the Christian religion, which is not dependent on such a primordial community? Tensions and possibly even contradictions appear unavoidable here. The secular, religiously neutral character of the state can hardly be acceptable to a religion of a *polis*. If, however, the form of the state's institutions is determined within a religious, political and cultural community, then, even if religious liberty exists for other religions, there arises at once the problem of the equality of citizens – without regard to their religion – in their legal and political rights, including access to public and political office, which is basic to a civil society.

The difficulties which exist at present in the state of Israel in formulating the list of fundamental rights to be included in the constitution are evident when Judaism is at the same time conceived as a political and cultural, as well as a religious community.

7   K.Marx, 'Zur Judenfrage I', in Marx, *Die Frühschriften*, Landshut (ed.), Stuttgart, 1953, p. 183.
8   R.Brubaker, 'Einwanderung und Nationalstaat in Frankreich und Deutschland', in *Der Staat* 28 (1989), pp. 1ff. (5).
9   E.-W.Böckenförde, 'Die Entstehung des Staates als Vorgang der Säkularisation', in Böckenförde, *Recht, Staat, Freiheit*, 1991, p. 112.
10 John Paul II, *Redemptor hominis*, nos. 10, 11; Speech at the General Audience on 21 February 1979. Published in German in *Osservatore Romano* on 2 March 1979, p. 2.
11 Klaus Schlaich, 'Der Öffentlichkeitsauftrag der Kirchen', in *Handbuch des Staatskirchenrechts* 2, Berlin, 1975, pp. 231–72 (251).
12 C.Schmitt, *Der Begriff des Politischen*, 3rd edn, Berlin, 1963, p. 26.
13 Second Vatican Council, *Constitution 'Lumen Gentium'*, no. 31.
14 Sermon in Limerick on 1 October 1979. Published in English in *Origins*, 1 November 1979 (vol. 9, no. 20) p. 324; see also E.-W.Böckenförde,

'Das neue politische Engagement der Kirche. Zur "politischen Theologie" Johannes Paul II', in *Stimmen der Zeit* 198 (1980), p. 219–234 (229).

SELECT BIBLIOGRAPHY

E.-W. Böckenförde, 'Staat, Gesellschaft, Kirche', in *Christlicher Glaube in moderner Gesellschaft* 15, Freiburg, 1982 (now also in *Schriften zu Staat, Gesellschaft, Kirche*, Bd 3, Freiburg, 1990 pp. 113–209.

Reflections on Religious Pluralism in Civil Societies

EDWARD SHILS

Our task is to analyze the conditions under which, in civil societies of a plurality of religious beliefs, the respective communities of these diverse religions can live in peace with each other, with mutual respect and with the attendant acceptance of the right of each religious community to enjoy freedom of religious expression and practice, freedom of religious association and freedom of religious instruction. We will be concerned here not so much with religious toleration in the sense of the readiness of the state to permit freedom and religious belief and worship to all or any religious communities but rather with the attitude of each of the religious communities within a civil society towards all the other religious communities in that same society.

A civil society has liberal and democratic features. The liberal features – the rule of law, freedom of the press, the freedom of association, assembly and petition, the separation of powers, freedom of private property, freedom of contract, and so on – are all part of our conception of civil society. The democratic features of liberal-democratic societies comprise an electorate extending to universal adult, male and female suffrage, parliamentary consideration of popular desires, mass political parties with administrative machinery of their own, direct elections of legislators, at least of the lower house, etc.

A civil society is more than this. It is a liberal-democratic society in which there is also a concern on the part of many members in many different parts of the society for the common good. Liberal-democratic society is a pluralistic society, with competition between groups; a liberal-democratic society is also a set of institutional arrangements to allow partisanship in attachment and the furtherance of the objectives of individuals and groups.

A civil society, however, is a liberal-democratic society in which partisanship, while permitted, fostered and facilitated, is also limited by civility. A civil society is one in which there is a collective consciousness of the whole society in which all the parts of the society participate.

Civility is expressed in sentiments of attachment to the whole of society and by decisions and actions which are concerned to protect and further the good of the whole society. This means that civility is an attachment of the institutions of the whole society, i.e., institutions like legislatures and the judiciary, which comprehend the institutions of the society and which can do justice to all parts of the society. It keeps in balance the various competing and conflicting parts of the society. The maintenance of balance among the parts enables the whole society to continue to function as a society and not simply as a by-product of the competition and conflicts of various parts of the society with each other.

A civil society is a variant of a liberal-democratic society: liberal-democratic societies may vary in their degree of civility. The institutions of a liberal-democratic society are the institutions of civil society, but the civil component of civil society is variable. A populist liberal-democratic society is not likely to be a civil society. By its stress on the superior merit of 'the people' and by the demagogy which flatters 'the people' and claims to speak on its behalf, by the rancour of its denunciation of the 'internal enemy', such as the wealthy, the bankers, the big cities, the 'interests' of ethnic and religious minorities, etc., it breaks the solidarity of society, excluding significant sections of the society from the collective self-consciousness.

The element of civility in a liberal-democratic society which is very highly stratified in status and in 'stratum-consciousness' (including class-consciousness), might also be weak. A very plutocratic liberal-democratic society is likely to be lacking in civility. A liberal-democratic society which excludes a large part of the population from participation – as the United States with respect to the black slaves and with respect to the black population between emancipation and the Second World War – is also a limited civil society. While the white population attained a fairly high degree of civility – within the limits of the ethnic boundary – American society in the periods in question was marked by a high degree of incivility with respect to its black members. British society of the eighteenth century was a civil society within the fairly narrow limits of the aristocracy and upper-middle classes of England, Scotland and Wales, with the exclusion of the lower strata of these three countries and most of the Catholic population of predominantly Catholic Ireland. The Republic of South Africa is, within the white section of the society of that country, often a civil society, but it is highly uncivil with respect to the black population. Similarly, India is a civil society in which civility is markedly restricted as far as the untouchable castes and the aborigines are concerned.

There may also be a civil element in oligarchical republics, in monarchical and even in tyrannical societies. In the latter, in which I include totalitarian societies, the civil element, to the extent to which it exists, is likely to be outside the centre of the society and it is likely to manifest itself primarily attitudinally and in opposition.

I

A civil society is not constituted solely by the ethos of civility. A society is a civil society when its members are also conscious of their membership in that society as a whole as well as in some of its multifarious communities or strata – religious, ethnic, political, doctrinal, etc. A civil society has its own traditions, relating to its history and its achievements as a society, its common institutions – political, judicial and legal, etc., – its common culture exhibited in a common language, a common body of literary works written in that language, and its common appreciation of certain momentous historical events and the greatness of certain historical personages.

A complex pattern of institutions is needed by civil society in order to cope in a civil manner with the problems raised by pluralities of beliefs, attachments and interests. Civility and its institutions exist to impose restraints on the aspirations of the diverse plural institutions which would otherwise be in unlimited conflict with each other, each seeking to increase its share of goods, services, status and influence. It could even be said that the institutions of civil society are called forth by the plurality of institutions; if there were not a plurality of beliefs, attachments and interests and the corresponding institutions, each pushing against the others, there would be less of a stimulus to the formation of civility and civil institutions. Civility is a form of constructive response to pluralism. But it is not the only response to pluralism; tyranny or repression is another response to pluralism. So are persecution, segregation and discrimination.

A pluralistic society in which rights of far-reaching autonomy are accorded to the various communities – and not only religious communities – and strata which make it up, may, in varying degrees, also be a civil society. A civil society is a pluralistic society in which the autonomy of its constituent communities and strata is qualified by the acceptance of obligations by individual citizens and groups of citizens to the society as a whole, to its particular organs and laws, and also to the ethos of civility. By the ethos of civility, I mean the practice of acting on behalf of the common good and of the general rule, in the making of decisions, of bearing in mind the consequences of the particular actions for the common good.

Consideration for the common good may coexist alongside

rivalry and competition for the ascendancy of one's own objectives. Where there is civility, the right of the others to exist, to be free and to adhere freely to their own beliefs and ideas, and to pursue their practical objectives is acknowledged as part of – but not the whole of – common good. Where this freedom exists, it is bound to produce conflict. Self-restraint and acknowledgement of the merits of the competing or conflicting rival are necessary to a civil society. This self-restraint might be the result of civil attachment to the whole society or a prudent calculation of costs and benefits. Such consideration for the other communities or strata within one's own society is often, but not always, a manifestation of attachment to the society as a whole and to the body of its citizenry. Thus while it is difficult to analyze the phenomenon of civility, one constituent is surely participation in a state of collective consciousness which extends to all or most of those human beings who live within the territory of that society. It is a sense of being a part – together with the other members of the society – of an entity of which the others are also part. Civility is a state of mind and a pattern of conduct, in which a section of the individual self is transformed into part of a collective self which then 'reaches into' and affects the individual self.

This solidarity with others in civil society may be generated or heightened by belief in a common descent from ancestors who possessed certain significant qualities which their living descendants possess by virtue of their ancestry. To share in ancestry is to share with living persons qualities or properties which the ancestors possessed.

This is one of the sources of the solidarity of a society. There are many other such sources but the sharing of a tradition received from predecessors who believed the same things as their descendants now believe is one of the most important of them. Sharing the same religious ancestors among contemporaneous believers of different religious communities can contribute to civility. It is obviously not enough.

II

Let us turn our attention to the phenomenon of religious toleration of different religious communities within a civil society.

Mutual tolerance of the major religious communities within a society might be a result of the prudent recognition by each that any effort on the part of one to suppress the other would give rise to a civil war with damaging consequences to itself and to its society. (This was one of the arguments for the toleration of dissenting religions in the seventeenth century.) Toleration and even fellow-feeling might be a result of a perception and appreciation that they each share certain traditions from which they derive some of the fundamentals of their respective beliefs. Even in the appreciation or understanding of universal religious propositions, the sharing of ancestry – even if only intellectual ancestry – creates a bond as it does in primordial collectivities which have a common biological ancestry. This common participation in a single religious ancestry and in the same doctrinal collective consciousness which it sustains, might inhibit the hostility towards the other party which is a competitor for the 'suffrage' of the faithful.

In any discussion of the relations between Christian and Jewish religious communities, the common traditions shared by Judaism and Christianity must be given much attention. Of course, not all Christian traditions are Jewish traditions and *vice-versa*. From the second century AD, at the latest, Judaism and Christianity became separate religions although both of them had their sources in Old Testament Judaism. Rabbinical and Talmudic Judaism acknowledged only traditions originating in the Old Testament. Christianity acknowledged selectively the traditions of the Old Testament and, more fully, those of the New Testament. With the establishment of the canonical status of the New Testament, Christianity was launched on a course of its own.

The strengthening of the common collective consciousness precipitated from the commonly shared tradition of the Old

Testament and of some of the traditions which arose in the two centuries prior to the lifetime of Jesus, could contribute to a greater solidarity of Jews and Christians. This greater solidarity might well inhibit the hostility fostered by the dominance or concentration on the traditions which separate them.

I have no disagreement with this view. But I would like to complement the analysis by referring to an additional factor which comes from life in a civil society. The tolerance of several religious communities towards each other, and, even more, the solidarity between then supported by the consciousness of sharing, up to a point, a common religious tradition, would be reinforced by the common collective consciousness of common membership in a civil society. At the same time, civility does not entail uniformity of belief; it does not obliterate attachment to any particular religious community and the religious tradition of that community. It would do so no more than political partisanship, and the espousal of divergent political, economic and social ideals or the pursuit of divergent economic interests are eradicated by civility. There is always some conflict between them but it is usually not severe. A state of tension is not the same as mutual exclusiveness in the relations between civility and attachment to divergent ideas and interests.

Nevertheless, civility is, in one sense, antithetical to attachment to a religious community; it is antithetical to attachment to a religious community where the latter claims exclusive, overriding and all-pervasive attachment, to the exclusion of any other attachment, whether religious or non-religious. There is another rather special sense in which civility and attachment to a religious community could be antithetical to each other. If we were to extend the meaning of civility to the point at which it is a part of a civil religion in which the civil society is the exclusive object of reverence and in which it is thought that the sacred is exhaustively embodied in society – this was Durkheim's view – then society as a whole and religious communities would be incompatible with each other, even if the population of that society were religiously homogenous. In that case, the society would be neither pluralistic nor civil. Nevertheless, even where the religious community does not strive to suppress its rivals and to replace the state by a hierocracy, there is still bound to be some tension between civil society and religious communities. These two instances of the antitheses of religious communities and civil societies are not representative of the normal cases of the relations of religious communities and society. That said, civil society and religious communities are frequently relatively conciliatory towards each other. As long as religious communities are devoted to a transcendent deity and a transcendent realm of which the deity is the centre and by which earthly life is to be guided, there is bound to be a conflict between attachment to the religious community and attachment to society. This would be true even where those who claim to represent the society do not sanctify it.

A civil society which makes modest claims on its citizens can come very close to the avoidance of conflicts with religious communities. Civil societies cannot avoid all conflicts with religious communities. This difficulty arises in part from the claims of religious communities, even those with moderate aspirations, to guide the familial and sexual conduct of their communicants and to some extent their economic conduct. It is about these connections that conflicts between civil societies and religious communities can occur.

III

Civility – the virtues which are part of membership in a civil society, particularly the virtue of caring for the common good, not just for the good of one's own or some other sector of the society – is not a religious phenomenon *per se*. It is not a religious phenomenon because it entails an attachment to an earthly institution, namely one's own society.

A society can have attributed to it properties of sacredness. It may be thought by its subjects or its rulers to be divinely ordained or inspired or legitimated. Such a society might be a theocracy – more properly called a hierocracy – but it can scarcely be a civil society nor one which encourages pluralism. A wholly sacred society cannot be pluralistic; a faintly, dimly, remotely sacred society can admit pluralistic structure. (Durkheim who thought that religious beliefs which were ostensibly about God were in fact beliefs about society to which transcendental properties were attributed, placed himself in a self-contradictory position regarding modern society. He thought that modern society was pluralistic as a result of its highly differentiated division of labour but being a society it had *ipso facto* to be sacred.) Theocracies – in fact, hierocracies – and divine kingships are uncongenial to pluralism and to the civility which under favourable conditions are supplements and qualifications to it.

In fact, however, neither the rulers nor the citizens of civil societies usually go so far as to proclaim themselves or their society to be divine or sacred and to be the proper and exclusive objects of worship. Nevertheless, there is some tincture of sacrality in any great aggregation of power and this offers an ever present ground for tension between the civil society and religious communities.

A society might be a civil society and not tend towards becoming the object of sociolatry or an idolized government. Yet, even then, there can be a point or zone of conflict in so far as the society legitimates itself entirely by a deistic or even agnostic rational law of nature which is therefore in conflict with a religious community adhering to a religion with claims to universal validity and worshipping a personal God who is the Creator of the universe.

Generally, the trend of modern civil societies and their authorities has been to refuse the establishment of particular religious communities even where establishment has been enshrined in the constitution; the exclusiveness of establishment is, in fact, refused. In other modern civil societies, church and state have been separated. Whatsoever the limitations of a complete separation, this is an attempt to create a civil society in which the attachment of the citizen to his fellow-citizens would be an attachment to them simply because they are his fellow-citizens and not because they are members of any particular religious community.

IV

Primordiality and its characteristic form of religiosity are very different from the communities and beliefs of universal religions. The success of the latter in the world has been gained at the expense of the former. Modern civil societies proclaim standards which are alleged to be inimical to primordiality – that is, to locality or restricted territoriality and to biological affinity and descent.

Primordial collectivities have their own religions. Where primordial societies flourished most their gods were frequently territorial – local – in their jurisdiction, and their members were linked with each other by ostensibly biological ties of ancestry and kinship. Primordiality has not been abolished in modern societies. It is often suppressed but it is not eradicated; it is often recrudescent. Primordial collectivities in modern societies tend to warp universal religions into their own patterns of belief. They tend to territorialize the gods of the universal religions, making them into the gods of a particular nationality or race.

They engender hostilities against religious communities which are not their own on the grounds that they are ethnically or nationally alien. Once the animosity is in play, it creates fictitious images of the ethnically alien religious community and its beliefs. This aggravates ethnically or nationalistically impelled hatred and legitimates it in the idiom of religious traditions.

In the presence of primordial – ethnic or national – attachments and the corresponding criteria of membership and evaluation, attachments to civil society and to the constituent role of the citizen, have a tendency to mollify antagonism and to muffle the clamorous voices of ethnic and nationalistic tendencies in the society.

V

A nationality is a collectivity which delineates itself by reference to its connection with a specific territory, by nativity in the territory or by descent from persons who were native to that territory. There are other properties of nationality – linguistic, cultural, traditional, etc., – but they too turn in considerable measure on the primordial phenomena of ancestral tradition and descent. Patriotism is attachment to nationality.

Civility entails nationality and patriotism, i.e., attachment to the inclusive, territorially bounded political entity, the name of which tends to be identical with the name of the territory. A civil society has a tendency to become a single nationality because of the territorial reference of the civil collective self-consciousness. Patriotism and nationality do not necessarily entail hostility towards other nationalities within the same society or towards other national societies or national states. Attachment to nationality does not by itself entail comparisons or conflicts with other nationalities. Given, however, the frequency of conflicts between states on behalf of their 'interests' (which might be only dynastic interests, or the interests of the governmental bureaucracy or of the military forces, but they might also be the economic interests of larger parts of the society) distrust, animosity and hostility often become associated with nationality or patriotism. Nationality becomes nationalism.

The externally directed hostilities and aversions of nationalism – as distinguished from the internal orientations and attachments of nationality – can often turn inward towards 'inner enemies', sections of the population which appear to be less national or to be connected with a foreign nationality. Persecution of the 'inner enemies' occurs and, short of those, discriminatory or unfavourable actions and attitudes towards them occur. These excrescences of nationality may be inhibited by civility.

Religious communities, even those which cut across the

boundaries of many nationalities, tend to 'nationalize' themselves; sometimes they become nationalistic and even racial. (There is a regression to primordiality when a given religion becomes markedly linked to a particular territory.

It may happen that one particular religious community regards itself as 'more national' than the others within the same society. This declaration of the inequality of the component nationalities of the various religious communities is a breach of civil obligation; it cannot but damage the relations between religious communities.

VI

Ethnicity is closely related to nationality. It refers primarily to a common biological lineage – usually fictitiously or ambiguously or both. Ethnic groups are primordial and for that reason they interpenetrate frequently with nationality, which is also primordial through its territorial reference.

It is in the nature of the communities of the universal religions that ethnicity is, in principle, irrelevant to membership in them. The universal religions, with the exception of Judaism, have divested themselves – again, in principle – of their primordial elements, attachment to a particular territory and biological lineage. Their gods, their interpretations of life and their moral rules are offered to all mankind.

Their freedom from ethnic attachment, from exclusive connection with any particular territory or any particular biological lineage makes them more competitive than primordial religions, which do not claim universal validity. This competitiveness for acknowledgement of superior validity is partly a consequence of the attenuation of ethnic connections; it is also paradoxically accentuated by doctrinally adventitious ethnic correlations. By this I mean that the geographical distribution of primordial properties is loosely correlated with the distribution of religious beliefs. For example, Christians are mainly Caucasian, or white, Buddhists are mainly Asian – Chinese, Korean, Japanese, Thai, Indochinese, Burmese and

Sinhalese. The lines of ethnic separation sometimes underscore the lines of separation of religious communities. Ethnic animosities accentuate the mutual distrust consequent to doctrinal and liturgical dissensus. The hatred of two ethnic groups for each other is reinforced or legitimated by their being of different religious beliefs which are in contention with each other over their claim to universal validity.

A diminution of hostility between religious communities might leave ethnic hostility without the support which it derives from the hostility between two religious communities, and might thus weaken it.

A diminution of the strain between the Christian and the Jewish religious communities could occur in consequence of an increased awareness on the part of each of the communities of their common religious tradition, and that diminution might also diminish the rancour between the ethnic communities which in many societies belong to different religious communities.

Ethnicity is inimical to civility. The strengthening of ethnic attachments weakens civil attachment. But it is important to emphasize that they are not invariably and irreconcilably incompatible with each other.

VII

Societies are also divided into different strata: the more powerful and the less powerful, with many intermediate strata, the wealthy and the poor, again with the numerous intermediate strata, managers and employees, strata of higher status and those of lower status, with many intermediate strata, and the educated and the uneducated, again with many gradations. These strata do not have sharply defined boundaries and individual and collective self-consciousness of location and attachment are very variable. The strata do not have such clearly defined boundaries as religious communities or even ethnic groups. There are also divisions between age-classes or generations and sexes.

Nevertheless in any particular situation some of the members of some of these strata bear grievances against some other strata in the same category. They attempt to hamper their aggrandizement or to aggrandize themselves *vis-à-vis* those against whom they have grievances. These conflicts are often conducted acrimoniously and violence sometimes occurs; they are, however, intermittent and participation in them seldom draws the entire category into the acrimony and violence. Even those who participate in these conflicts are not wholly absorbed in them.

The lines of separation among these various strata – although they are frequently vague and unstable – often coincide approximately with lines separating religious communities, ethnic communities, etc. This increases the harshness and unconciliatoriness of the conflicting bodies. The conflicts of religious communities are aggravated when boundaries of religious communities coincide approximately with the boundaries of social strata.

There are also lines of cleavage among political groups within civil society. (There are of course political conflicts in uncivil societies but they are often conducted secretly or are confined to a small minority of the population.) In civil societies, which afford freedom of expression and association, and open competition among parties contending for the highest places of political authority, the lines of political conflict sometimes coincide with the lines of religious separation. Such coincidences aggravate relations between religious communities.

As against all these separations, in a society which is pluralistic with regard to religious confessions and communities, political groups and parties, and in economic organization, and is ethnically heterogeneous too, the civility of society is all that performs the functions of a governor, preventing centrifugal tendencies from breaking the unity needed to keep the society functioning in a moderately effective way.

Perception of the benefits of exchange for each of the parties to a transaction, awareness of dependence on the satisfaction of the demands of others as a precondition for the satisfaction of one's own demands – in brief, 'interests' – are certainly also important for maintaining a society in an orderly condition. Similarly, fear of superior powers also has an ordering function. Routine, reiterative or stereotyped, more or less habitual behaviour has a similar ordering function. Without the kind of collective consciousness, vague in content but always reaffirming the value of the society as a whole – what I call civility – a society is in danger of fissure along many lines. This is especially so in a society which has become, like modern Western societies, publicly pluralistic, in which there is a demand that the centre become accessible and responsive while individual and collective rights to autonomy have become entrenched, and their proponents and beneficiaries are constantly seeking to expand them.

Without civility, a pluralistic society might become deadlocked and incapable of actions which are needed; or it might become so entangled in conflicts that the law of the stronger prevails without challenge or moderation. It might decay into a war of each against all or into a tyranny which offers order and internal peace at the cost of suppression.

Yet, these last conditions are rather exceptional. Most societies avoid them most of the time. Might it therefore not be said that in a chronic state of nature or in a condition of continuously oppressive and coercive tyranny, all the societies which have existed for extended periods, must have been civil societies? The answer is emphatically no, but the question deserves serious consideration.

VIII

A civil society is only one of many kinds of society. What is unique to civil society and why is it the type of society which has best served the human race in the conditions which were in operation in the nineteenth and in the twentieth century and in some parts of the world – mainly Western Europe, North America, the Antipodes? And why has it from time to time from the last decades of the nineteenth century been held up as a model in Latin America, Africa and Asia?

A civil society is a pluralistic society but all large societies are pluralistic in the sense that they have consisted of more or less autonomous segments. The ancient Near Eastern empires, the Roman empire, the Chinese empire, were all pluralistic societies in this sense. In none of these was the central authority, the king or emperor, able, with the aid of whatever staff of administrators and soldiers he could muster, to control all of the society over which he ruled. The rulers were on the whole content with the pluralism, *de facto*, of their kingdoms or empires. There was little they could do about it. In any case, their main objectives were the collection of taxes and tribute, the levy of soldiers and the avoidance of active resistance to their authority at those particular points, where they sought to exercise it.

The absolutist monarchs of the seventeenth and eighteenth centuries went as far as the technology of administration and transportation permitted, although the extent of their success should not be exaggerated. Many pockets of autonomy existed despite efforts to bring them under the control of the central government. Lords in their estates, chambers of merchants and the heads of families maintained some of their traditional autonomy, despite the growing comprehensiveness and pervasiveness of legislation and administrative decrees.

It was only in the twentieth century that some rulers in a few important countries attempted to obliterate all the pluralism of autonomous communities and areas in their societies. In the Communist societies in the Soviet Union, Eastern Europe and China, in the Fascist regime in Italy and the National Socialist regime in Germany, strenuous efforts were made by the ruling party and its organs to bring under a single all-comprehensive pattern of authority the innumerable specialized professional, occupational, industrial, commercial collectivities, all of the technology of communication at a distance, all cultural, scientific, educational and religious institutions, and all local and regional organizations. Voluntary conformity impelled by belief in the legitimacy of a strong authority, fear of the coercive action of the police, anticipation of benefits in money, appointments, and status from submission to the demands of the rulers and their agents, supported by a pervasive system of internal espionage, permitted the suppression of the strong tendency towards pluralism of the highly differentiated societies in which these totalitarian regimes were established.

It is a characteristic of totalitarian societies, particularly the Fascist and National Socialist variants, that they recognized the tendencies toward pluralism through the organization of an extremely elaborated set of functional organizations of occupation and professions and their corresponding institutions in their attempts to bring under their control all cultural institutions such as academies, universities, etc. They did not obliterate these institutions; they allowed them to go on with their traditional activities but they made deep inroads into them in numerous ways which were more than symbolic. They adapted themselves to pluralism by coercive repression.

IX

A pluralistic society is not necessarily a civil society. In most large societies, there remains a pluralism of primordial communities, local and familial-*cum*-religious. Large societies have also called forth a certain degree of division of labour with its associated development of specialized mercantile, industrial and handicrafts activities. Each of these developed and nurtured its own traditions which reinforced collective self-consciousness of each of these groups.

In large-scale traditional societies – mainly monarchies and empires – these groups developed their own internal life, controlling admission to membership, promulgating guiding rules of conduct of their members, etc., and acquiring acknowledgement, either by statute or custom, of their own procedures and arrangements.

The societies in which this pluralism existed were not civil societies. They had no public political life. The centre of the society – the crown and the court – were in some respects self-contained. They were immune from the influence of the periphery; they had little interest in the beliefs and activities of the peripheries of their realms. They had, in the main, little institutional provision for the representation of the desires, actual or imputed; in the latter case they were trans-figured as 'interests'. There was a marked tendency for decisions to be deliberated and made within a very small circle and for most of the adult population not to be consulted about what those decisions should be. Public discussion of those decisions, before or while they were being considered and after as well, was slight in the numbers who partici-pated in it and in the intensity and concentration of that dis-cussion.

In ancient and early modern republics the radius of civility was very short; in monarchies and empires, if they did have senates or other elected assemblies, it was also very small.

The opportunity for civility is given by the existence of a civil society. This does not mean that civility cannot exist in societies which are not civil societies. When it does occur in such circumstances, it is, however, an unusual event. The virtue of civility requires a civil society for its exercise, just as a civil society needs the virtue of civility. It was only in the nineteenth century that civil societies came into a more or less full existence. The establishment of freedom for the expression of divergent points of view and for the exposition of accounts of the condition of society, the toleration of a plurality of religions, a legal order which assured some justice to individuals whatever their status, the legal existence of a plurality of political parties free to canvass an extended electorate, the cessation of the legal exclusion of members of religious and ethnic minorities from educational opportuni-ties and public offices, the existence of a press, daily and periodical and free to discuss problems thought to be of importance to the society and to criticize the measures taken by governments recommended by the opposition, the publicity of debate in representative legislative bodies and of the reports of special investigative commissions – all created a civil society. With these developments, there emerged the role of the citizen as a full member of the political society and as the bearer of a share in the responsibility for the society as a whole.

IV

PERSPECTIVES AND ACHIEVEMENTS

The New Gnosticism: The Book of Exodus as an Ideology

RABBI LEON KLENICKI

The theology of liberation is an attempt by contemporary Christian theologians to relieve the poverty and oppression of Latin America and the Third World. It is a noble cause with an ignoble methodology. The theology of liberation uses the Biblical text as an ideological pretext to disregard Judaism after the Exodus from Egypt. Justifying their philosophy of social change and revolution they overlook and ignore one of the most miraculous triumphs of liberation in all of history: the return of the Jewish people to their promised land, Israel.

Liberation theologians present themselves as the most advanced and radical Christian thinkers. But their denial of Zionism as an example of liberation and their determination to see Judaism solely as the preparation for the coming of Christianity echoes the Medieval Christian contempt for Judaism. I see it as part of a new Gnosticism.

Biblical Faith and Ideology: The Challenge of a New Gnosticism

Gnosticism, which is a generic term for a variety of religious movements of the first centuries of the present era, has been revived today through the use of theological interpretations of the book of Exodus. The new Gnosticism summons tradition to justify social trends for a 'radical' comprehension of God's design.

Gnosticism is known from Jewish and Christian sources and most recently from the Nag Hammadi, a collection of Gnostic books found in 1945 in Egypt. The two most common themes in Gnostic thought are the creation of the world as a perversion of the divine plan and the role of Jesus as the bearer of the message of deliverance from the world of matter. In the New Testament Gnostic, the expectation is that Jesus will accomplish God's purpose for the Creation. Persian dualism influenced Gnosticism picturing God and an adversary, Satan, in an eternal conflict, with the world divided into a kingdom of darkness and a realm of light. The Dead Sea Scrolls illustrate this Gnostic concept by stressing 'esoteric knowledge' as a key to redemption, enabling an élite to preach the abyss separating the human from the divine (Thanksgiving Psalms, IQH11, 13–14).

According to Gnosticism, the world is a prison from which human beings want to escape. Deliverance is the dissolution of the worldly aspect of the soul and liberation from the burden of the universe. It is the destruction of the old world and the passage to the new. The instrument of salvation is knowledge – Gnosis itself, aware of humanity's imprisonment. For the most part in modern times, Gnosticism has been out of fashion. Recently, the old Gnosticism has reappeared in new forms.

Reading the Word of God

The exponents of the new Gnosticism rooted in Jewish and Christian hopes for redemption began by reading a basic text inspired by contemporary ideologies. They read the Hebrew Bible, trying to overcome a 'realm of darkness', a kingdom of injustice and poverty, in order to achieve social perfection.

Gnosticism follows the tradition of commentary and interpretation. These systems entail two routes to understanding. One penetrates the text itself from the inside to discover its meanings. The other, the typological route, works from the outside to project into the text itself concerns that are not necessarily inherent in it. The text then becomes a pretext for points of view superimposed upon it.

Textual interpretation from the inside is the natural tool for Biblical study and rabbinic understanding. It is part of the Jewish experience of God and the covenantal relationship. Simon Rawidowicz explains its central meaning as follows:

Explicatio and *commentatio* follow the 'text' step by step, uncover and explain it from the aspect of its form and content, language and historical background. *Interpretatio* is centered on the 'soul' of the text, its leitmotif, its main purpose, its essence, its particular character. *Interpretatio* assumes that there is a hidden layer in both the 'form' and the 'content' of the document to be interpretated; this 'hidden' needs uncovering. There is a mystery between the words and between the lines, that which the document ought to have said and did not say, either because it could not say (for various reasons) or it did not want to say – this it is which intrigues the interpretator (*sic*) who will naturally dig in the hidden layers of the 'text'. He wants to make the implicit in the text explicit, to 'spell out' that which is implied.[1]

Times of crisis, which renew the energies of a people, as Rawidowicz points out, inspire new approaches and interpretation. Crisis, in this sense, has to be understood as a turning-point in history. In Judaism, the Babylonian exile is a good example, 586 Before the Common Era (BCE which is how Jews refer to the period likewise called BC, Before Christ). The historical experience of abandonment and of return to the promised land, led Jews to an awareness of new dimensions in the God–Israel relationship which required interpretation. By commenting, interpreting and expounding upon Biblical text, Ezra and Nehemiah attempted to solve the national identity crisis. Their interpretation emerged from the text itself. The rabbinic literature, from the *Mishnah* and *Midrash* to the *Talmudim*, from Jerusalem and Babylonian, testify to the process of historical and theological awareness of God in each generation.

On the other hand, interpretation as a projection from outside onto the Biblical text also appears frequently during times of crisis for reasons related to historical events or to the inner problems of the commentator himself. Explanations that do not necessarily belong to the text itself are projected onto the Bible in order to justify various theological or ideological beliefs. The Jewish experience has been that such interpretative projections tend to diminish the meaning of Judaism and the centrality of Israel in God's purpose. Judaism has confronted this problem from its earliest days; this problem has been posed, for example, by Hellenism, Roman culture, Gnosticism, Christianity and even psychoanalysis (as exemplified by Sigmund Freud's comments on Moses and the Jewish religion).

A special form of the projective method of interpreting the Biblical text from outside is Christian typology. The word 'typology' derives from the Greek *tupos*, meaning model or impression. A type is the ideal of the genus or species; it has come to mean an individual who typifies or embodies this ideal. However, in interpreting the Bible, the *Tanach*, Christian interpreters used the typological method to give their assertions a special twist. The people and incidents in the story of the ancient Israelites became signs and symbols for anticipating coming events, specifically the advent of Jesus. Thus Christian typology presents Biblical Judaism as the prologue to Jesus and Christianity. The vocation of Judaism is to prepare the way to Jesus's mission. The reference of Jeremiah 31, 31 to a new covenant is interpreted Christologically as a reference to Jesus as the 'New Testament', as the renewed covenant of God. The Sinai covenant, God–Israel, is considered 'completed' by Jesus and Christianity. This interpretation has promoted what has been called by Professor Jules Isaac, in his study on the subject, the teaching of contempt.

Professor Isaac discerns this contempt in the way in which Christians have taught about the dispersion of the Jews, viewing it as a providential punishment for the degenerate state of Judaism at the time of Jesus and the crime of deicide.[2] Some of these concepts have been denied by contemporary

Christian documents on Judaism though they still linger in present ideological Christian interpretations of the Bible, especially of the book of Exodus. This ideological reading and interpretation protects the projection of concepts alien to the original text.

The Ideological Reading

The word 'ideology' was coined by Destutt de Tracy in his *Projet d'Elements d'Idéologie* (1801) to describe a group of French philosophers who were the theorists for Napoleon and his system. A general definition of ideology according to Webster's dictionary is 'a systematic scheme or co-ordinative body of ideas or concepts, especially about human life or culture'. The most specific definition for our purposes is that ideology is a system of ideas concerning phenomena, especially of social phenomena; it is a manner of thought characteristic of a radical group or political tendency.

This system of ideas has a specific social significance when it is applied to the understanding of contemporary society and the world. It is an application of certain theological ideas for the promotion of social solidarity and the integration of values.

Ideology is an interpretative system of political ideas embodying and giving concrete form to the more abstract set of values. It is an argument for a policy or a social movement which because of its claim to justification by some transcendent morality (for example, history), provides legitimacy for its programme and a commitment to action in the effort to realize those beliefs.

Twentieth-century ideologies are represented in a wide variety of political beliefs; in religious thinking, ideology has become a Messianic vision. Religious ideology considers the Hebrew Bible and the New Testament as basic documents for a particular social philosophy and the interpretation of modern life.[3]

The Politicization of Religion: A Biblical View

The *Tanach*, the Hebrew Bible, is critical of political adventures that damage the religious life of the individual and the community by diminishing their ethical duties. Two examples are significant. Books I and II of Samuel, and I of Kings, Books 1–12, illustrate the confrontation between religion and politics that pervaded Judaism for centuries.

I Samuel 9, 15–17 speaks of God as initiating the monarchy, and commanding the prophet to anoint Saul as King. But God gave only a grudging consent to the community's demand which is described as a rebellious rejection of God as crown and king of the universe (I Samuel 8, 6–9).

These two attitudes, approval and rejection, were present in the prophetic view of state and society. The prophets were sensitive to the needs of royal politics and international relations, but they were equally conscious, and their remarks made the people aware of this, of the duties imposed by the covenantal relationship. The revelation at Sinai, the foundation-stone of Israel, established standards of conduct that the king and the state, representing the Hebrew people, were under obligation to follow. The state was not a tool of religion or a religious bureaucracy, but part of God's covenant with Israel.

Prophetic criticism was not related to any political party. It was a denunciation of social evils, poverty and hunger, and of syncretism arising from the acceptance of foreign fashions. Social evils were transgressions of the Sinai alliance. The prophets blamed king and state for fostering pagan influences and ways, and for failing to follow the obligations of the Sinai agreement. They castigated their kings for not fulfilling their mission as anointed of God. The criticism was not a social denunciation, but a critical consideration of a failure of religious responsibility *vis-à-vis* the God–Israel covenant and its obligations.

The prophets called for repentance, for a return to God for inspiration and a renewal of the covenantal link. The

Teshuvah, both repentance and an answer to the situation of transgression, was a call to reconsideration of political actions that would open the gates of hope, a national renewal in the promised land and a renewal of individual spirituality.

Present day understandings of the prophetic message wrongly emphasize the prophetic denunciations as part of a revolution directed to change the society of their day. Theologians of liberation in particular follow this line of thought, adapting typologically a figure of the past to present political situations. Contemporary religious criticism has taken a prophetic overtone but rarely, or never, the prophetic concern for the covenantal rupture, which is the source of all social evils. The prophets denounce poverty and the exploitation of widows and orphans as transgressions of God's covenant and Israel's obligation to take care of the poor. The prophetic view was critical of the failure to obey the law of covenantal God–Israel moral obligation. It was not an ideological or political criticism. The prophetic tone of today's theologians of liberation, however, is disguised by a methodology basically alien to the Biblical source.

Theology as an Ideology of Liberation: The New Typology

Today's new typological interpretation has emerged as a response to social crisis which challenges Christianity as well as Judaism. It is the challenge of poverty and injurious social conditions. Times of crisis and tension originate spiritual answers in response to historical challenges, in the spirit of a tradition, or in the adaptation of a spiritual heritage to new perspectives. This has been the reality of rabbinic Judaism and Maimonides in Judaism, or Saint Thomas Aquinas and Richard Niebuhr in Christianity. Many present responses are framed by ideology, the Gnosticism of the twentieth century. Theology is transformed into ideology, the ideology of liberation.[4]

Theology has not followed the deep, essential changes in

thought and scholarship that make out of the twentieth century a unique moment in the development of human intelligence. In general, theology has remained within the Medieval framework, constraining the growth of human spirituality and understanding of God.

Reactions have varied. One group of theologians searches for a non-theistic concept of God through process theology, revising the language describing God and religious existence. Another group looks for a meaningful theology expressing social and political concerns. One tendency, following extreme conservatism, adapts classical Thomist theology to the defence of a particular social order. Another, arising in poor societies, denounces social injustice, exploitation and poverty.

The radical trend does not emphasize the science of God. It stresses the interpretation of life and the world in a socially redemptive way. Third World theologians from Africa, the Far East and Latin America, lay emphasis on the existential social situation; they are closely associated with political movements whose goals are to transform society. Theology becomes another form of ideology, proclaiming the idea of a social revolution. This does not mean that poverty and social injustice should not be denounced. It is our religious obligation to denounce evil, hunger, poverty, following the covenantal obligation to feed the poor. However, the proclamation of a 'preferential option for the poor' by theologians of liberation is not the solution to poverty. It is just giving the hungry man a fish without teaching him how to fish. The real obligation of religious people is to open economic opportunities; sources of work for the 'have-nots' of the world. Otherwise we merely have the childish satisfaction of destroying a structure without building anything better to take its place.[5]

The theology of liberation is representative of this mood of Christian thought. Latin America has contributed the major movement of thought that developed from Father Gustavo Gutierrez, *A Theology of Liberation: History, Politics and*

Salvation,[6] which is already a classic in the field. The author is a Peruvian priest, teaching at the Catholic university in Lima, who lectures often in the United States and Europe. His book has been translated into many languages.

Father Gutierrez bases his theological thought upon the book of Exodus, the story of Israel's delivery from Egyptian bondage. The Biblical text narrates the story of the Jewish struggle for political and spiritual liberation, for the humanization of their condition. The epic of the Exodus of the Jewish people is seen by Father Gutierrez as a historical process with 'an element of capital importance: the need and the place for man's active participation in the building of society' (p. 158). The lesson of the Exodus experience is set out in this manner:

To work, to transform this world, is to become a man and to build the human community; it is also to save. Likewise, to struggle against misery and exploitation and to build a just society is already to be part of the saving action. Which is moving toward its complete fulfilment. All this means that building the temporal city is not simply a state of humanization or pre-evangelization, as was held in theology up until a few years ago. Rather, it is to become part of a salvationary process which embraces the whole of man in all human history. Any theological reflection on human work and social praxis ought to be rooted in this fundamental affirmation. (pp. 159–60.)

Father Gutierrez defines the meaning of liberation in terms of Christian religious experience. Man, the master of his own destiny, lives in a situation of poverty and underdevelopment that oppresses him both psychologically and materially. Liberation means the aspiration for a better society, but also an understanding of history, a 'conscientification' of a tragic historical situation and the human being's responsibility for a better destiny. Father Gutierrez sums up his approach by saying that:

to conceive history as a process of the liberation of man is to consider freedom as a spiritual conquest; it is to understand that the step from an abstract to a real freedom is not taken without a struggle against the forces that oppress man, a struggle full of pitfalls, detours and temptations to run away. The goal is not only better living conditions, a radical change of structure, a social revolution; it is much more; a continuous creation, never ending, of a new way to be a man, a permanent cultural revolution.

From a Jewish perspective, Gutierrez's interpretation of Exodus is one-sided. It lacks any knowledge of rabbinic thought or contemporary Jewish religious thought. Gutierrez states that the Exodus was a 'political act of God', a process of liberation in itself. Judaism recognizes that it was a movement of liberation, but argues that the liberation from Egyptian bondage became meaningful only when Israel received God's teaching, Torah, at Mount Sinai, and the promised land. The process that starts with Moses taking an enslaved community out of Egypt culminated with the spiritual liberation of Israel at Mount Sinai, and in Eretz Israel, the land of Israel.

Neither Father Gutierrez nor any other exponent of the theology of liberation refers to the state of Israel and its struggle for liberation. Theologians of liberation are interested in contemporary movements that foster liberation, yet with the exception of Jürgen Moltmann, they disregard Zionism as the theology of liberation *par excellence*. Gutierrez reads the Bible in a selective way. He and his fellow-thinkers take the first nineteen chapters of Exodus as a typology of liberation. Genesis 12, the promise of land, the very origin of Zionism, is not considered at all. Zionism is not a contemporary political creation. It is part of the Jewish faith and commitment and it is evident in daily prayer and rituals. Jews recall the promised land in the Passover liturgy, a celebration of inner and outer freedom culminating in God's revelation at Mount Sinai.

The theology of liberation neglects this aspect of Judaism. It does not mention Zionism as noted, as the liberation movement *par excellence* in the twentieth century. This neglect is part of the 'teaching of contempt', denying Judaism and the Jewish people a role in God's design. The church Fathers denied the Jewish people a place in God's scheme of salvation.

The theology of liberation denies the Jewish people a role in history. The Jews do not count; they are not part of history, unless they are victims of the Holocaust.

Reading the theology of liberation, one has the impression that the Jewish people disappeared after leaving Egypt. Many references are made to liberation in Latin America and the Third World but the authors remain silent about the contemporary struggles of the Jewish people. They do not mention the conditions of Protestant denominations in Latin America either. Both Jews and Protestants are in general considered second-class citizens there. In some countries, like Argentina, non-Catholics have to register as members of 'foreign cults'. The same country constitutionally requires that the president and vice-president be Catholics. Liberation theologians pay no attention to Jewish contributions to the good of society. There are comments on Jewish participation in the creation of the Latin American trade union movement. This was done at a time when the church denounced these attempts as inspired by anarchism or Moscow. Liberation theologians have little memory for the history of social progress on the continent.

Liberation thought has paid no attention to the Holocaust. An exception is Gustavo Gutierrez's book on *Job: God-Talk and the Suffering of the Innocent* (New York, 1987). He refers, however, to the Holocaust in a typological manner. Jewish suffering is compared to the social injustice of Latin America. But this comparison is outrageous. Poor people can be helped through social change and political opportunity. For the Jews in Nazi Europe there were no opportunities. Jews were condemned to destruction simply because they were Jewish. Father Gutierrez does not see or want to see this point:

The reason is that in Latin America we are still experiencing every day the violation of human rights, murder, and the torture we find so blameworthy in the Jewish Holocaust of World War II. Our task here is to find the words with which to talk about God in the midst of the starvation of millions, the humiliation of races regarded as inferior, discrimination against women, especially women who are poor, systematic social injustice, a persistent high rate of infant mortality, those who simply 'disappear' or are deprived of their freedom, the sufferings of peoples who are struggling for their right to live, the exiles and the refugees, terrorism of every kind, and the corpse-filled common graves of Ayacucho. What we deal with is not the past but, unfortunately, a cruel present and a dark tunnel with no apparent end.

The old 'teaching of contempt', the heritage of the church Fathers, is also present in the Latin American theology of liberation in the work of Juan Luis Segundo, Leonardo Boff and Enrique D. Dussel. Segundo, for example, in his book *Jesus of Nazareth: Yesterday and Today* refers to Judaism in Volumes 1 and 2. His chapters are called 'The Lie of the Law', 'Sin, Enslaver of Judaism' and so forth. The titles speak for themselves.[7] Enrique D. Dussel in his *El Humanismo Semita*, written on a *kibbutz* in Israel, ends his book by inviting Judaism to convert to Christianity in order to achieve total meaning. The text was written after Vatican II *Nostra Aetate* 14.[8] It follows, however, a Medieval idea which denies a vocation to Israel. Leonardo Boff in his book on Christology echoes the same Medieval contempt. It is amazing that a theologian well-versed in contemporary philosophy and theology, Marxism and psychology, remains a disciple of the church Fathers in his consideration of Jews and Judaism. He writes in his *Passion of Christ, Passion of the World: The Facts, Their Interpretation and Their Meaning Yesterday and Today* (New York, 1987):

The Jews' rejection of Jesus, their strategems, will be seen as a hardening of their hearts, a refusal to hear the voice of God speaking through Jesus. A scrupulous observance of the law, in the interest of ensuring one's salvation, had made the people forget God, the author of the law and of salvation. The Pharisees were particularly observant of the letter of the law, and terrorized the people with the same scrupulosity (*sic*). The Pharisees contemptuously referred to the people as 'this lot, that knows nothing about the Law', and dismissed them as 'lost' (John 7, 49). Legally the Pharisees were letter-perfect. But underneath lurked a fundamental wickedness, and Jesus tore away their disguise: 'You pay tithes on mint and herbs and seeds while neglecting the weightier matters of the law, justice and mercy and good faith' (Matthew 23,

23). Instead of furthering liberation, the law had become a prison with golden bars.

The writings of this liberation theologian are imprisoned in the triumphalistic thinking of the Medieval church. Leonardo Boff disregards or ignores present New Testament research that show Jesus's criticism of the Pharisees as part of the Pharisaic movement. Jesus was stating a critical view already known in the rabbinic circles of his days.

Reading Exodus: The Gnostic Temptation

The book of Exodus is now at the heart of contemporary theology. The text has become for many Jews and Christians a point of departure for ideological explanations.

In his *Exodus and Revolution*, Michael Walzer starts his commentary by stating that he will expound it as 'a paradigm of revolutionary politics'. He adds that:

Without the new ideas of oppression and corruption, without the sense of injustice, without moral revulsion, neither Exodus nor revolution would be possible. In a text as we have it, the new ideas are shadowed by their older opposites: the sense of injustice by resignation, revulsion by longing. The shadows are sharply drawn; this is part of the realism of the Biblical story. But it is the new ideas that make the new event. They provide the energy of the Exodus, and they define not only for the deliverance of Israel, but for all later interpretations and applications of that deliverance. Henceforth, any move toward Egypt is a 'going back' in moral time and space. When Milton wrote of the English in 1660 that they were 'chosing them back for Egypt', he did not mean to describe a mere return (or a cyclical repetition) but a retrogression a 'backsliding' to bondage and corruption . . . This slide is not incomprehensible, for Egypt is a complex reality . . . But it is a defeat. It is a paradigm of revolutionary defeat.[9]

This comment is typical of a present approach that emphasizes revolution, praxis, action in history. It disregards two main points. One is the presence and action of God as liberator. The second, that the book of Exodus does not end with Chapter 19. It continues by focusing on the inner liberation of the spirit emphasizing the reality and obligations of the covenantal relationship, emphasizing a way to acknowledge God by sanctifying everyday existence through ritual and prayer.

The acceptance of God's command inaugurates a new time. It is the beginning of inner liberation, a cleansing of physical and spiritual slavery. To be liberated implies to go free politically but following a way, a path retracing in daily action the reality of the covenantal relationship. This will be the response of the people of Israel in the process of *Teshuvah*, the return to God. They will accept the reality that they are a people with a mission: *Am Segulah*, a people to witness God.

NOTES

[1] S. Rawidowicz, *Studies in Jewish Thought*, Philadelphia, 1974, pp. 47–8.

[2] J. Isaac, *The Teaching of Contempt*, New York, 1964.

[3] J.B. Thompson, *Studies in the Theory of Ideology*, Berkeley, 1984, pp. 194–204.

[4] For the Christian critique of ideological interpretation see J. Ellul, *Jesus and Marx: From Gospel to Ideology*, Grand Rapids, 1988.

[5] R.H. Neuhaus, (ed.) *The Preferential Option for the Poor*, Grand Rapids, 1988.

[6] Gustavo Gutierrez, *A Theology of Liberation*, New York, 1973.

[7] Juan Luis Segundo, *El Hombre de Hoy Ante Jesus de Nazaret* I and II, Madrid, 1982.

[8] E.D. Dussel, *El Humanismo Semita*, Buenos Aires, 1969.

[9] It is also reflected in two recent interpretations written by Jews involved in liberation thought. Both require a deeper knowledge of Jewish sources. D. Cohn-Sherbok, *On Earth As It Is In Heaven, Jews, Christians and Liberation Theology*, New York, 1987. M.H. Ellis, *Toward a Jewish Theology of Liberation*, New York, 1987.

Jewish–Christian Relations: Achievements and Unfinished Agenda

PIETRO ROSSANO

The tension and the complementarity of plurality and unity is among the most fundamental human experiences, which can be found highly expressed in a symphony, in a liturgical celebration, as well as in silent contemplation or in active involvement in the life of the society, in the *polis*.

The references to 'pluralism' in *Gravissimum educationis munus* 6 and to 'pluralistic society' in *Gaudium et spes* 76 (the terms used in the Second Vatican Council) seem to relate to the contemporary experience, without particular philosophical or theological implications. The declaration on religious freedom excluded every form of external pressure in regard to religious creeds (*Dignitatis humanae* 2), and elsewhere it is clearly affirmed that the church is not linked to one particular form of human culture and can enter in communion with every culture (*Gaudium et spes* 42, 58).

The coexistence of particularity and plurality is a characteristic feature of thought in the Western world, and not only in the Western. Since 'the beginning' (*Bereshit*, Gn. 1, 1; John 1, 1) the Bible presents to us the Holy One and the glory of His magnificent and various Creation. *The Rigveda* praises the One from which all things came into being (x, 129).

Both the Jewish and Christian traditions gave witness to the theological concept of pluralism, and to its cultural implications. The Jewish reflection on the written *Torah* considered the 'Living teaching' of God as the first creature: 'The Lord created me at the beginning of his work' (Prov. 8, 22) and developed the monument of the 'oral *Torah*'.

The Talmud is the best example of the pluralistic attitude of Jewish culture. A preparation for the Christian tradition has been the *Wisdom of Solomon*, a script that can be seen also as a Passover commentary, in which it is affirmed: 'a multitude of wise men is the salvation of the world, and a sensible King is the stability of his people' (6, 24). Here the message of redemption, in its Jewish substance, is expressed by the cultural mediation of the Hellenistic culture. A positive attitude towards plurality can be seen in the words of Jesus in the gospels: 'He who is not against us is on our side' (Mark 9, 40).

Sometimes we think that the origins of Christianity and the Middle Ages were without real pluralism. Allow me to mention a few of the many examples of the pluralistic attitude of the ancients. The philosopher and martyr, St Justin, whose theory of the *lógoi spermatikoi* permitted him to be appreciative and receptive of the wisdom of the ancient Greeks: St Augustine in the Latin tradition spoke of the *rationes seminales* present in the whole universe as many sources of truth.

St Bonaventure is an outstanding witness of the Medieval doctrine of the three books containing divine revelation: *liber naturae, liber scripturae, liber vitae*, the last of them being accessible to everyone, Christians and non-Christians alike.[1] It is interesting to note that the famous *Nathan der Weise* of Lessing has its antecedent in the novel of Boccaccio on *Melkisedek, the Jew and Saladin*.[2]

More committed is the famous essay of Raymond Lull, *De tribus sapientibus et infideli*. Passing through Thomas More and Nicolaus of Cusa[3] we reach Henry Newman who in *The Development of Christian Doctrine* compares the church among the religious traditions older than herself to the infant Jesus seated in the Jerusalem temple among the doctors '*audientem illos et interrogantem eos*' (Luke 8, 2).[4]

This philosophical, theological and cultural background

of 'pluralism' in its larger sense must be recalled to better understand the seriousness of the Christian attitude towards Jews and Judaism after the Second Vatican Council and its declaration *Nostra aetate* 4.

Achievements

Since this survey is not primarily academic, I will assume here that we are all aware of the history of the development of Jewish–Christian relations in this century and especially after the Second Vatican Council. Consequently I will limit myself to presenting a systematical overview of the achievements, as I see them, from a theoretical perspective.[5]

It seems to me that the first achievement – from the Christian point of view – can be indicated in the acknowledgement of the 'other' (and this term is rich with the philosophical–religious implications evoked by Emanuel Levinas), the Jew, as 'our brother in the faith of Abraham' (John Paul II, 31 December 1986). Related to this is the other affirmation that the Old Covenant was 'never revoked by God' (John Paul II, 17 November 1980).

From this principal point flow many consequences. These include the consciousness of the distinct and peculiar religious identity of the Jews, 'beyond any syncretism and any ambiguous appropriation' (John Paul II, 13 April 1986). They also include the offering of the 'respect and love' due to the Jews (Paul VI, *Ecclesiam suam*, 1964). Another consequence, parallel and complementary to the first, is 'the clarity and affirmation of our Christian identity' (John Paul II, 6 March 1982). If we would have a serious dialogue, it implies a serious presentation of our doctrine on Christology and on Ecclesiology, with particular reference to the two documents: *Bible et Christologie* (Pontifical Biblical Commission) and *In hac relatione* (International Theological Commission). Closely related to the preceding points, is the Council's affirmation concerning the 'spiritual link' and 'the spiritual patrimony common to Christians and Jews' (*Nostra aetate* 4). It is a common bond that does not destroy but strengthens the two communities and their individual members in their specific differences and in their common values. As elements of this common bond, following Cardinal Martini's enumeration, I quote: the faith of Abraham and of the Patriarchs; the vocation to holiness; the veneration of the sacred Scriptures; the tradition of prayer; obedience to the moral law of the Commandments; the witness to God by the 'sanctification of the name' and respect and responsibility for all creatures, commitment to justice and peace.

A practical consequence – perhaps the most important – of these theoretical principles, is the clear consciousness of the necessity of our dialogue as an essential instrument in our relations. This dialogue, encouraged by the Council, has acquired many dimensions; within the general religious perspective we develop also many others: historical, social, etc.

Four other major achievements must be listed. They are relevant both from the conceptual and the practical point of view. The first achievement is the condemnation of anti-Semitism and commitment against it, already strongly expressed by the Holy See in 1928. It is not only important to condemn but also – or much more – to elaborate the theological, philosophical and juridical reasons for such a condemnation.[6]

The second major achievement is the clarification concerning the historical and the theological responsibility for the Passion and death of Jesus Christ made in many documents since *Nostra aetate* (in the *Guidelines* issued in 1974 and the *Notes* issued in 1985). It has been declared that historically there did not exist either collective responsibility or collective guilt. Theologically, it was explained, the cause for the Passion and death are the sins of all humanity. The best overview was proposed by John Paul II during the general audience of 28 September 1988.

Thirdly, the acknowledgement that the *Shoah*, the catastrophic genocide of the majority of European Jews, has a particular religious value in the eyes of Jews and Christians alike. We are committed to remembering and avoiding the opposite risks of banalization or of de-judaization, in order to prevent other genocides.[7] And last, but not least, Christians recognize the relevance of the land of Israel in the religious life of the Jewish people. It is significant that after the Council the first three meetings of the International Catholic–Jewish Liaison Committee were dedicated to this argument (Paris 1971, Marseille 1972, Antwerp 1973). Concerning the state of Israel, the *Notes* published in 1985 affirm: 'The existence of the state of Israel ... should be envisaged ... in reference to the common principles of international law.'

I would also recall, in this list of achievements, the sweeping changes, as regards the Jews, in the universal prayer which the church raises to God on Good Friday. Instead of the cancelled *pro perfidis Judaeis* we have: 'For the Jews, who were the first listeners to the Word of God, the church asks progress in the love of God and fidelity to the Alliance.' If we consider that for a Catholic the *lex orandi* becomes *lex credendi*, there is here a basic achievement which will have a long-term influence on the whole church.

Let me conclude this long list of positive achievements by referring to two sets of concrete realizations:

Many institutional arrangements were established at various levels everywhere in the world. The most important, chronologically, were: in 1946, the International Council of Christians and Jews (ICCJ); in 1966, the 'Service de Documentation Judeo-Chrétien' (SIDIC); in 1970, the International Catholic–Jewish Liaison Committee (ILC); in 1974, the Holy See's Commission for Religious Relations with Jews. In addition to this, various academic centres for Judaeo-Christian studies were created at Seton Hall, Lucerne and Jerusalem, etc.

The World Council of Churches (WCC), and other churches and ecclesiastical communities, have during these forty years issued many important documents, encouraging the development of Christian–Jewish relations.

In the Catholic Church the pontificate of John Paul II is

characterized by an intense personal effort for promoting the dialogue at every level.

Agenda

First of all, I would stress the importance of prayer. We have recent good examples: the prayer during the visit of the Pope to the Roman Synagogue (1986), the prayer for peace in Assisi (27 October 1986). We can praise the Lord for the gifts of inspiration from the first leaders of the dialogue, Pope John XXIII, Jules Isaac, Augustin Bea, Joseph Lichten, Zachariah Shuster and many others. We can ask for His assistance, for our conversion and reconciliation according to Biblical teaching (see *Dives in Misericordia* III, 4). In the *qaddish*, as well as in the Lord's Prayer and in the *Magnificat*, we pray: 'Our Father, Hallowed be thy Name, Thy Kingdom come'.

Another important point must be our effort to achieve obedience to God's will and to God's plan of Redemption. We, Jews and Christians, are called by God in the sacred Scriptures to be *holy people* dedicated to God (Ex 19, 6; 1 Pt. 2, 9 – *goy qadosh*, *ethnos agion*). We must be repentant communities of faith, faithful to the truth, to our respective religious traditions, but at the same time open to learn about the religious tradition and history of others. We have a common commitment, witness and responsibility, since we share so many spiritual treasures of faith: 'Both Jews and Christians carry out the service towards the rest of mankind ... This service constitutes a *priestly* ministry, a mission that can unite us without confusing us with one another until the Messiah will come. He whom we invoke Maranatha!'[8]

Along these lines we must seize the opportunity to continue and develop, in its integrity, our religious dialogue, as the Pope wrote to Archbishop John May (8 August 1987): 'The more we try to be faithful in loving obedience to the God of the Covenant, the Creator and Saviour, contemplating in prayer his wonderful plan of redemption and loving our neighbour as ourselves, the deeper will be the roots of our dialogue and the more abundant its results.' This dialogue can be conducted on theological, exegetical, cultural themes, in the appropriate circles or institutions, but must also be disseminated and extended to the various levels of our communities, in order to overcome 'the residues of indifference, resistance and suspicion that may still prevail in some sections of our communities'.[9]

We hope practical cooperation will flourish in many fields of human life as a result of this dialogue. We hope that it will result in a common action for justice and peace, according to the exigencies proclaimed by the prophets that we venerate in the holy Scriptures. This should lead to particular activity against racism, discrimination and anti-Semitism; to a serious commitment to the promotion and defence of human life and rights and the integrity of creation. With particular regard to the last Apostolic Letter of John Paul II *Mulieris dignitatem*, I would stress our common reference to Genesis 1–2 for the family in the world of today. We share particular concern for the young people and for educational problems. We should increase our efforts in pastoral and catechetical action, according to the suggestions of the last document of the Holy See.[10] In the social field, John Paul II recently recommended, in his encyclical *Sollicitudo rei socialis* (VII, 47), a special cooperation between Jews and Christians, and extended this appeal also to the Muslims.

Let me quote another point of the programme of the ILC, jointly agreed in 1985: 'To undertake a joint study of the historical events and theological implications of the extermination of the Jews of Europe during World War II (frequently called the Holocaust or, in Hebrew, *Shoah*)'.[11] In this context we are confident that the Centre of Auschwitz – a centre for prayer, study and education – will be realized according to the programme promulgated in Geneva 22 February 1987. For such realization the support of the European churches is of course necessary.

In conclusion, a last point could be that: in the Holy Land, the land of Patriarchs and Prophets, where Jesus Christ lived, died and has risen, where Muslims go to accomplish their holy pilgrimage, where Jews have been living in the state of Israel, for forty years now, we hope for an improvement in the dialogue of peace among all members of the Christian, Jewish and Muslim communities. From these relations of friendship and confidence on the basis of their faith, I hope and wish that a positive contribution to a true and complete peace may result. When all these points of our 'unfinished agenda' are realized, what will be the future? I am deeply persuaded that the Bible – both Jewish and Christian – is at the root of Western civilization and it represents an irreplaceable source of inspiration for the future of mankind. Two major tasks seem to be incumbent on Christians and Jews today in our pluralistic society: to face the risks of technocracy with all its positive and negative implications, and to enter into dialogue with the religious traditions of Asia (Jerusalem with Benares). In this perspective it seems urgent that the Jewish–Christian dialogue expand itself into a trialogue which would include the Muslims. There are signs, seeds and hopes for this everywhere in the world. Only on this condition would we be able to make a relevant contribution, in our pluralistic technological society, to humanize technology and to meet our brothers of Asia, waiting for and hastening to the day of peace, justice and light announced by our Prophets (Is. 66, 18–23).

NOTES

[1] St Bonaventure, *Quaestiones disputatae de mysterio Trinitatis*, Pars I, art. 2.

[2] G. Boccaccio, *Decamerone* I, 3.

[3] See Thomas More, *Utopia* (II, Religions of the Utopians); Nicolaus von Cues, *De pace fidei*.

[4] J. H. Newman, *An Essay on the Development of Christian Doctrine* (1985) II, 8, 2.

[5] For further details I refer to the recent book *Fifteen Years of Catholic–*

Jewish Dialogue, published by the Libreria Editrice Vaticana and by the Libreria Editrice Lateranense, Romé 1988, and to the article by Cardinal J.Willebrands in *L'Osservatore Romano* 24 March, 1988, p. 6. See also Cardinal Martini's paper delivered at the Workshop on Anti-Semitism, Princeton Theological Seminary, Philadelphia, 1–2 May 1988.

[6] On this subject see J.Willebrands, *The Church facing Modern Anti-Semitism* (Lecture delivered at the University of Aberdeen, 17 October 1988).

[7] On this point see J.Fisher, *John Paul II on the Shoah*, Washington DC, 1988.

[8] See Card. Martini, paper cited above.

[9] From the ILC Programme, cf. *Fifteen Years of Dialogue*, p. XIX.

[10] See *Notes*, 1985.

[11] See *Fifteen Years of Dialogue*, p. XIX.